HOW TO WORK FOR A CHARITY

On a Paid or Voluntary Basis

By Jan Brownfoot & Frances Wilks

A Directory of Social Change Publication

**How to Work for a Charity:
on a paid or voluntary basis**

By Jan Brownfoot and Frances Wilks

First published in 1994

Copyright © 1994, Directory of Social Change
The Directory of Social Change is a registered educational
charity, Charity No. 800517

No part of this book may be stored on a retrieval system or
reproduced in any form whatsoever without prior
permission in writing from the publisher.

Designed and typeset by Linda Parker
Printed and bound by Page Bros, Norwich

ISBN 1-873860-17-X

contents

Acknowledgements 4

Introduction 5

Chapter 1: Finding Your Way around the Voluntary Sector 7

Chapter 2: Identifying the Right Job for YOU 25

Chapter 3: Becoming a Volunteer 35

Chapter 4: Setting about Getting Paid Employment 47

Chapter 5: Getting a First Job – Opportunities for Young People 63

Chapter 6: Employee Volunteering and Secondment 79

Chapter 7: Returning to Work – Opportunities and Options 87

Chapter 8: After Redundancy – Opportunities and Options 99

Chapter 9: After Retirement – Opportunities and Options 107

Chapter 10: Working and Volunteering Overseas 115

Chapter 11: Guidelines and Opportunities for People with Disabilities 133

Chapter 12: Advice Giving, Counselling and Working on a
           Telephone Helpline 151

Chapter 13: Starting Your Own Organisation 163

Chapter 14: Becoming a Trustee 173

Chapter 15: Volunteering in a Charity Shop 181

Appendix 1: Assessing Your Skills and Attributes 187

Appendix 2: How to Write a successful CV 189

acknowledgements

The publication of this book and its companion volume, *The Directory of Volunteer and Employment Opportunities*, was made possible through the generous sponsorship of Whitbread PLC and with a grant from the Voluntary Services Unit of the Home Office. The publishers are grateful for this support for the encouragement of volunteering and for the provision of better information on employment opportunities in the charity sector.

Over half the chapters in this book are based on a series of information and guidance leaflets on Routes into Volunteering and Employment with charities and voluntary organisations that was specially produced for Charityfair 93, the national Charity Exhibition held annually at the Business Design Centre. The leaflets have been amended and added to for this guide. We would particularly like to thank the following for their contributions and help:

- **Lauren Bates** of CR Charity Recruitment;
- **Anne Booth** of Birmingham Disability Resource Unit;
- **Paul Farmer** of the Samaritans;
- **Keith Galpin** of REACH, Retired Executives Action Clearing House;
- **Cathy Harden** of British Executive Service Overseas (BESO);
- **John Nurse** of Voluntary Service Overseas (VSO);
- **Gill Sargeant** of the Industrial Society;
- **Elaine Willis** of the Volunteer Centre UK.

We would also like to thank all the people who shared with us their experiences, whether as paid workers or as volunteers in the voluntary sector, and who allowed us to quote from our interviews with them to illustrate the major points in this book. Thanks are also due to the many organisations that sent us information, answered questions and provided guidance and suggestions of various kinds.

INTRODUCTION

> **"** I wanted to work in the voluntary sector because I grew tired of the profit-making ethos of business. Working for a charity is very rewarding and great fun, but it's also hard work and you need commitment. Getting the right advice at the beginning and having boundless enthusiasm definitely help! **"**

> **"** I volunteered overseas in my year off because I wanted to see another country and another culture, and experience things I wouldn't do again. **"**

Maybe you've felt or feel similarly?

- Do you want to change careers and work for a cause you believe in?
- Have you been bringing up a family or caring for a relative and want to return to work in a similarly caring/sharing environment?
- Are you unemployed, perhaps because of redundancy, or because you are a newly qualified young person in the Catch 22 of no experience – no job, no job – no experience?
- Perhaps you have recently retired but would like to go on making a useful contribution to society?
- Are you keen to understand how people from a different country, culture and background live and work?
- Does a demanding and worthwhile challenge interest you?

If your answer to any of these questions is 'yes', then this book is for you. It represents the distilled practical experience of a number of people who have, either by choice or chance, come to work in the voluntary sector. It has been produced specifically to assist people from many diverse backgrounds to find work, whether paid or unpaid, with a voluntary organisation.

We ourselves have gone through this process. This book, and the accompanying *"Directory of Volunteer and Employment Opportunities"*, are part of the fruit of it. After contrasting experience in the commercial world – in market research and the media – we met on the *Working for a Charity* course. This gave us the necessary basic information about voluntary organisations and put into focus the voluntary work that we had both been doing for most of our adult lives. It also confirmed our feelings that we wanted to work in the voluntary sector ourselves. We believe this is a particularly exciting time to be joining it.

There are several reasons for this. The world of work is changing; many people now switch jobs to take up new careers, perhaps with different ways of working. Far more of us are living longer and are seeking enjoyable and active ways of contributing to society. Many people are without paid work – volunteering can be an excellent way of getting useful experience for a CV (Curriculum Vitae) and gaining self-confidence. Furthermore, various Government policies are transferring many of the services previously carried out by the statutory sector into the voluntary sector, which is changing rapidly and developing to accommodate its new role.

One final word – the key to all this is commitment. Once you have committed yourself to working in the voluntary sector, whether it be to a paid job or volunteering, and to any of the many causes, you will find all sorts of challenges and rewards flow from it. Commitment and taking that first step with courage can bring fulfilment that you couldn't have foreseen.

As Goethe says:

"Whatever you can do,
Or dream you can, begin it.
Boldness has genius
Power and magic in it."

Jan Brownfoot and **Frances Wilks**

1
FINDING YOUR WAY AROUND THE VOLUNTARY SECTOR

WHAT IS THE VOLUNTARY SECTOR?

To work effectively in the Voluntary Sector, whether in a paid or unpaid capacity, you need to understand it. It is different from

- the Commercial or Private Sector which operates for profit, and
- the Statutory Sector which consists of government and official bodies providing services.

What makes the Voluntary Sector different? The historical background, its organisational systems and methods of working, the way it is funded, and the legal and ethical principles which underlie it, all help to determine the particular nature of the culture and structure of the voluntary sector today.

> **"** *On the whole the Voluntary Sector lacks the organisational rigidity of the corporate sector. It means that there is less consistency in procedure and chain of command. Much more is left to the enterprise of the individual. I find this challenging.* **"**
> Sheenagh Day, Fundraising Manager, Family Planning Association

Currently the voluntary sector is undergoing great change. Government policies such as care in the community and privatisation of services are putting new and greater demands and responsibilities on voluntary organisations. The dismantling of much of the welfare state means they are becoming more important and more significant in Britain than they have ever been. You may be aware of the on-going debate concerning the role of the state and what services should be provided by public bodies and what through voluntary effort.

The voluntary sector as a whole now provides many basic services, sometimes in competition with the public and private sectors. And this is likely to remain the case, whatever the political colour of the government. At the same time many statutory services and organisations including schools, hospitals and museums are being re-formed as independent and voluntary-managed bodies. But, given that the voluntary sector's turnover is estimated to be around £16 billion a year compared with £130 billion for the public sector's expenditure on health and welfare, charity, as you can see, cannot replace the state. However, it can compliment and supplement state provision, and can respond faster to needs and new demands.

There are specific advantages to working in the voluntary sector. As it is relatively unstructured it is possible to achieve aims and objectives quickly and develop aspects of your job that appeal to you and that you enjoy. Also it offers opportunity for personal development due to the many challenges available. As a working mother I appreciate the flexible working patterns more easily available in the voluntary sector and the non-hierarchical management structure.

Pam Smith, London First

Britain's voluntary sector is bigger in size than the country's agricultural sector. It covers a wide range of independent organisations which operate on a not-for-profit basis. There are about 500,000 altogether (with 170,357 of them registered as charities in 1992). They include:

- **voluntary organisations** – bodies run by voluntary management committees
- **charities** – bodies run by voluntary management groups which have charitable status
- **self-help groups** – run by voluntary committees for the benefit of their members, rather than the general public. Because there is no public benefit, these cannot be charities
- **informal clubs, associations and societies** – which represent the largest part of the voluntary sector

- **non-governmental organisations** (NGOs) – a United Nations term covering non-statutory bodies generally

Whatever their particular type, to the 'person in the street' voluntary organisations are thought of as 'someone who would like your money' and 'where you feel it will be well spent'.

The main features of voluntary organisations are:

- they are cause-led
- they are set up by concerned individuals
- they are non profit-making
- each operates through a constitution
- committees of volunteers control them

Although these similarities provide common links, there are also many differences, notably in their activities, their size, where they operate (local, national, overseas), who runs them and how they are funded.

Types of Voluntary Organisations

You will find almost every kind and variety of activity and interest represented in the voluntary sector. Organisations have been set up concerned with virtually everything to do with humans, animals, the environment, the world and more. You name the subject area, there's almost certain to be an organisation of some kind to do something about it. People see a gap in provision or a need which they want to fill or do something about. As a result new agencies are constantly being formed. Conversely others close down, perhaps because the purposes for which they existed are no longer valid or their original aims have been fulfilled or because they have just run out of steam or money. But the general trend is that the number of voluntary organisations is increasing.

You may already realise that voluntary organisations come in all sizes as well as types. They can be:

- very **big**, rivalling medium to large private sector companies in their 'annual turnover' and the number of staff they employ
- very **small**, literally 'one man and a dog'
- something **in between**

Some start small, perhaps because a few committed people cared about a problem. This was the case with the **National Trust**, the **Spastics Society** and the **Alzheimer's Disease Society**, all of which became national organisations in time. Some stay small, perhaps fulfilling a vital local need, such as a local hospice (like the **St Nicholas Hospice** in Bury St Edmunds, Suffolk), a preservation project or a specialist museum. Some like the Ironbridge Gorge Museum Trust in Shropshire grow in importance and stature with their success. A few form part of an international network concerned with issues such as the environment (like **Greenpeace**), or human rights (like **Amnesty International**). Some protect the rights of their members professionally; others campaign to change the law on matters such as homelessness or prison reform.

What a voluntary organisation can do is determined very much by the size and nature of its funding. Voluntary organisations are run and funded in a multiplicity of ways.

SOME EXAMPLES OF VOLUNTARY ORGANISATIONS

- **Animals** – Blue Cross, Pets as Therapy, Royal Society for the Prevention of Cruelty to Animals (RSPCA)
- **Caring/Counselling** – Crossroads, Jewish Care, The Samaritans
- **Children** – The Children's Society, The Girl Guides, National Childminding Association (NCMA)
- **Education** – Eton, The Dyslexia Institute, Workers Educational Association (WEA)
- **Elderly People** – The Abbeyfield Society, Centre for Policy on Ageing (CPA), National Benevolent Fund for the Aged (NBFA)
- **Environment/Conservation** – Action with Communities in Rural England (ACRE), Friends of the Earth, Inland Waterways Association
- **Health/Medicine** – ASH (Action on Smoking and Health), Down's Syndrome Association, St John Ambulance
- **Overseas** – Christian Aid, The Ockenden Venture, Tools for Self Reliance
- **Recreation** – Association of Railway Preservation Societies, UK Sports Association, Youth Hostels Association (YHA)
- **Religious Affairs** – Scripture Union, TOC H, Union of Muslim Organisations of UK and Eire
- **Women** – Junior League of London (JLL), The National Council of Women of Great Britain (NCW), Womankind (Worldwide)

They may:

- get by on an entirely voluntary basis using the efforts of their volunteers and with virtually no funds at all
- charge membership fees or subscriptions
- raise funds through all manner of methods e.g. holding fetes, organising fun runs, rattling tins, having television appeals, perhaps employing professional staff to do much of the work
- get individuals to covenant money
- get grants towards the work
- get endowments or legacies which can provide them with investment income.

Sometimes a voluntary organisation has services it can sell to raise money. A hostel for the homeless, for example, charges its residents for bed space and these charges are picked up through the Social Security system. A museum may make an admission charge or a theatre charge for tickets. There are also many types of grants available from government, trusts and private companies (including sponsorship as well as donations). Many voluntary agencies use more than one method of raising funding.

However, much fundraising depends on public generosity and good will. Many voluntary organisations are now in competition with each other for what may be a decreasing amount of public and private money. You have probably also heard of the term 'compassion fatigue', the result of too many requests for support being made. Lotteries, however, can be a successful way of getting people to continue giving, and the advent of the National Lottery could bring much needed extra funding into the voluntary sector.

> The top five fundraising organisations are the National Trust, Oxfam, Royal National Lifeboat Institution, Imperial Cancer Research Fund and the Cancer Research Campaign. Each raises in excess of £40 million each year from donations, legacies and fundraising.

What is the difference between a Charity and a Voluntary Organisation?

There is a very important difference of definition between the various organisations that make up the voluntary sector. You can have a voluntary organisation which is not a charity (e.g. campaigning bodies, self-help groups like tenants associations, sports clubs), but you cannot have a charity which is not a voluntary organisation.

The definition of 'what is a charity' is legal and historical, being based on the Statute of Elizabeth, an Act of Parliament of 1601. The Act gave the protection of the State to private sources of funding established for the public benefit. Today the working definition of a charity is a body set up for public benefit for purposes defined as charitable by law.

These purposes and the definition have been altered or extended since 1601 by an evolving body of law. In the 1890s Lord Macnaghten, a leading judge, ruled that there were four types or 'heads' of charity:

- trusts for the **relief of poverty and distress**
- trusts for the **advancement of education** for public benefit
- trusts for the **advancement of religion** for public benefit
- trusts for **other purposes beneficial to the community**

The last category is a 'catch-all' and changing one which in the 1990s incorporates organisations that a few years ago would not have been included (e.g. charities for better race relations or for people with HIV/Aids). For an organisation to be a 'charity' there must be some sort of 'public benefit' in its aims. An enclosed order of nuns was once refused charitable status on the basis that there was no public benefit, although the nuns claimed that the intercessionary prayers that they offered up did constitute a public benefit.

Any organisation in England and Wales wishing to be a charity applies to the **Charity Commission** for charitable status, and must adhere to the requirements laid down in the 1992 and 1993 Charities Acts. The Charity Commission is required to monitor charities to see that they are operating properly and spending their money effectively. In Scotland and Northern Ireland there is no formal registration procedure for charities, so organisations usually apply to the Inland Revenue for registered charitable status.

What can and can't a Charity do?

There are certain things which charities cannot do within the definition what is 'charitable'. For example a charity cannot exist purely for political purposes and cannot be party political. Also a charity cannot undertake purely commercial activity. Charities, however, can and do campaign as part of their work.

Each charity sets out its purpose or **objects** in a constitution, which then defines its policy and area of work. The objects may be very wide or very narrow, and the area of work very local or even international. The **trustees** (who must normally be unpaid) form the committee of management to run the charity and have to work within the constitution to fulfil the objects. The objects, which may have been laid down many years ago, have to be interpreted in the light of current conditions and needs. If a charity wants to amend its objects in any way, it will normally have to apply to the Charity Commission or the Court.

There are many different types of charities addressing a huge range of purposes and objects. They fall basically into two main types:

- those that **give** because they have money (usually called an endowment) to invest. These are known as 'Trusts' or 'Foundations'
- those that **do**, perhaps providing a service or campaigning, (either by using their own assets or by raising funds).

There are also many voluntary organisations that don't bother to apply for charitable status. Those that do register gain various benefits. These include tax and rate relief, as well as simply being able to say that they *are* a charity – which can greatly help fundraising and grant applications!

> In 1992 there were 170,357 registered charities in England and Wales and 4,681 new charities being created that year.

The Legal Structure of Voluntary Organisations

Whether charitable or not, all voluntary organisations have a legal status, being either:

- **Unincorporated** – where the organisation *does not* have any legal personality of its own so that those who run it personally have to enter into any agreements or contracts and are personally liable if anything goes wrong – or
- **Incorporated** – where the organisation *does* have a legal personality of its own. This is the case with those set up as companies limited by guarantee, where the liability of the trustees is limited to a nominal sum

Members of the managing committee or the trustees usually form the Board which runs the organisation's affairs (*for more on Trustees see Chapter 14*). This committee:

- oversees the **work**
- manages the **income**
- determines **priorities**
- makes the main **decisions**.

It retains responsibility but can decide whether to delegate tasks to paid staff or to use volunteers, whether to set up sub-committees or do everything itself. Many voluntary organisations would welcome approaches from people with relevant skills or experience who are interested in serving as a committee member. Committee members or trustees cannot be paid, but can be reimbursed for out-of-pocket expenses.

Apart from volunteering in this way, many voluntary organisations use volunteers to do other work. Some of the types of opportunities available are outlined below. If you want to become involved in the voluntary sector, you may find that volunteering for an organisation of your choice is the best way to make that first step. Alternatively, if you want or need paid work, you could investigate the possibilities of employment. Or if you see a need or a gap in provision you could set up your own organisation.

Employment Opportunities

The types of paid and voluntary jobs available in voluntary organisations are as diverse and wide-ranging as the sector itself, and are expanding as voluntary organisations adapt to meet new government policies, and changing social and economic conditions.

> **"** I am a general Jack of all Trades – administrator, social worker, informal counsellor, fundraiser, public relations person, volunteer co-ordinator. You name it, I've done it. Even cleaned the toilets when the cleaner was off ! **"**
>
> Trisha Ward, Co-ordinator, Holocaust Survivors Centre

If you look at advertisements in papers such as The Guardian, The Independent, The Voice and other more specialist publications (such as Community Care and Disability News) for employment opportunities in the voluntary sector, you will find the variety as great as that in the commercial sector. Of course not all voluntary organisations are large enough to have the range of departments which a private sector company or a statutory body may have. But some are. In smaller organisations, staff may have to 'double up', perhaps doing more than one job and utilising a range of skills.

Whatever the circumstances of any one organisation, across the voluntary sector generally jobs can be found in finance, public relations, marketing, administration, research, advice/counselling and clerical, to name a few. Many organisations

> **"** I trained to be a chartered accountant. After I qualified in 1991 I started to look around at the possible career paths I could follow. At about the same time a number of articles appeared in newspapers and magazines about professional people moving into the voluntary sector. The idea of using my skills for a non-profit goal particularly appealed to me. My current job was advertised in The Guardian. The person specification said qualified or part-qualified accountant **essential** and experience of the voluntary sector **desirable. "**
>
> Elise McGreevy, Head of Finance and Administration, Crisis

also need specialist staff from such backgrounds as science, medicine or education. Some jobs require previous training or experience, others may require the appropriate skills with training provided as part of the induction process.

A random sampling of national advertisements for jobs in the voluntary sector during summer 1993 revealed a wide range of positions and opportunities, from top level posts at over £40,000 a year to part-time work (15 hours weekly) at around £7,000 pro rata. They included:

- a Director for two different charitable trusts
- a Head of Research and Information for a Third World agency
- a Health Co-ordinator within a religious organisation
- a Personnel Officer in an international development agency
- a part-time Organiser for a children's charity
- a Development Worker for an HIV/Aids organisation
- a Manager of Direct Marketing in an overseas charity
- a Housing Officer with a Christian housing group
- a Disability Worker on a woman's project
- a Fund Raiser for a health care charity
- a Systems Support Assistant for a campaigning charity

Many organisations also advertise in local papers, and some may only advertise locally, particularly for part-time positions, those below senior management level and clerical work. Before you decide precisely what you want to apply for it is worth reading through a variety of advertisements to see the sorts of skills required, the sort of previous experience that is felt to be desirable, the expectations that voluntary sector organisations have of their staff, and the kinds of salaries paid. You might also spot an opportunity or see an organisation you would like to become involved with on a voluntary or informal basis; this could lead on to paid employment later. Voluntary organisations with their own newsletters usually advertise job opportunities in these too. It is worthwhile looking through the newsletters of those organisations which you are particularly interested in.

EXAMPLES OF TYPES OF JOBS NEEDED IN VOLUNTARY ORGANISATIONS

- Activities Organiser
- Actor
- Administrator
- Accountant
- Animal Inspector
- Care Assistant
- Carer
- Child Protection Officer
- Clerical Worker
- Consultant (*various*)
- Co-ordinator

- Counsellor
- Dog Trainer
- Fundraiser
- Housing worker
- Instructor
- Linguist
- Manager (*various e.g. appeals, building, shop, stage*)
- Nurse
- Office Worker

- Project Worker
- Researcher
- Rehabilitation Worker
- Secretary
- Shop Assistant
- Social Worker
- Supervisor
- Telephone Canvasser
- Therapist
- Veterinary Surgeon
- Youth Trainer

Administrative and secretarial work is a basic requirement for all voluntary organisations. Many local organisations, some local branches of national organisations and small national agencies are run by a single administrator or co-ordinator, perhaps working with part-time support staff. To ensure that you can take advantage of any opportunities that may arise for these jobs, you need to have or get at least competent word processing skills. These will come in useful anyway whatever the work you may do. Another possibility to explore is seasonal employment. Whether in charity Christmas card shops, running holiday schemes for disabled children or organising seasonal play schemes, you could find interesting opportunities for short-term employment.

> **"** I presented myself at my local Citizens Advice Bureau (CAB) as a potential volunteer adviser. I did the basic training course and joined a team of about ten advisers led by a part-time organiser. When she retired I became a salaried joint organiser and then eventually sole manager. In 1992 I retired as manager and reverted back to being a volunteer again. **"**
>
> Joan Price, CAB worker

VOLUNTEERING OPPORTUNITIES

There is great freedom in the UK for anyone to set up and promote their own voluntary organisation. This gives the sector vitality and constant growth and provides numerous opportunities for volunteering. It also means that if you cannot find something to suit you and there is a cause you believe in, you can start doing something yourself on a voluntary basis. Your efforts might even attract people to the cause, leading you to set up your own organisation – and you might eventually even get paid employment from it. But be warned, starting a voluntary organisation needs enormous commitment, a great deal of vision, an enduring belief in the cause and a lot of hard work. See *Chapter 13* for more details on starting your own organisation.

How to begin Volunteering

You may feel it is more realistic and sensible to volunteer for an established organisation, at least to begin with. So how do you find out what is available in your area? You should be able to get information from a number of different sources. These include:

- Your **local library** and the **local authority** (council). They should have lists of the different kinds of organisations which will help you decide what activity you would most like to volunteer for and who to get in touch with.

- A **Volunteer Bureau** or a **Council for Voluntary Service** (CVS) office. Contact them and tell them what type of activity you would like to be involved with, what you can offer, and when, and for how long you are available. They will either have existing opportunities or they will endeavour to find the kind of volunteer position you are looking for.

- A specific national **voluntary organisation**. Contact its local office or, if it doesn't have one, contact head office. Ask whether it uses volunteers and, if so, in what ways help is needed and whether it is actively recruiting. Even if it does not have opportunities currently it may have in the future or it may be able to suggest other similar organisations that you could approach.

> *I saw an article about RSVP (Retired Senior Volunteer Programme) and wrote to them. I was interviewed and they offered me a job as Area Organiser. I find jobs in the community for people over the age of 50 and retired to do voluntary work, and I find the volunteers. The oldest person I have at the moment is 82. She volunteers in a primary school. She is the school 'granny' – the kids will talk to her but not to their own parents. She's enjoying it – it's keeping her young. RSVP has no age limit – you can go on till you drop! There is no problem finding placements for people. The problem is finding the volunteers. Many older people fear they won't be able to make a contribution. But there is something that everyone can do.*
>
> Alan Brown, Area Organiser for RSVP, CSV

There are also national organisations that can advise or that have volunteering schemes of their own:

- The **Volunteer Centre UK** produces leaflets on many aspects of being a volunteer and is also building up a data base, 'Signposts', listing volunteer opportunities around the country. You can ask the Centre for a printout of the types of organisations working in your area and their needs for volunteers.

- **Community Service Volunteers** (CSV) creates opportunities for people to work as volunteers in their own communities. Volunteers – CSVs – may be young or retired, working or unemployed. They can be graduates, school students and school leavers, professionals, homeless people.

Some are young offenders recruited from adult open prisons; others are disadvantaged. CSV believes everyone has something to offer and gives everyone the chance to volunteer, whatever their background or age.

- The CSV **Retired Senior Volunteer Programme** (RSVP) targets people over 50, partly or fully retired, who want to fill their lives actively and positively. It is volunteer-led, using a nation-wide network of area organisers, who find the opportunities and recruit interested people. **REACH** (Retired Executives Action Clearing House) offers a placement service for the retired and early retired who are looking for a second career as a volunteer.

Volunteer work done by Community Service Volunteers, CSVs, including older RSVP volunteers, may be in schools, hospitals or museums. It can involve visiting the sick or housebound, providing respite care and support for carers, teaching basic skills to young people leaving care, or helping to protect the environment. Schools and hospitals frequently need volunteers. In one girls school that had no librarian two

> *" After recovering from an operation, a friend suggested RSVP to me. I became a volunteer coordinator for Hertfordshire. I cycled my old push-bike 160 miles back from the first RSVP conference I attended in Bristol. Sponsorship money I raised amounted to £700, which I donated to our newly-formed local hospice. I now have a team caring for the gardens there. Another project I'm involved with is 'Swimming for the Disabled' with 16 members and several swimming coaches who give their time to RSVP, about two hours a week. If I have any foreign students to stay, I take them to see an elderly couple who speak six languages between them."*
>
> Tigger Hewitt, Volunteer Organiser for RSVP, CSV

RSVP volunteers set up the library, organised the indexing system and, together with other volunteers, lent the books. In other schools RSVP and CSV volunteers help students with reading, cookery lessons, learning foreign languages, and go on outings with them. Others respond to the needs of organisations like the **RNLI** or **Macmillan Nurses** for help rattling tins for fund raising appeals.

Organisations like the Volunteer Centre and CSV can provide you with numerous examples of opportunities for volunteering. Another source of information is *The Directory of Volunteer and Employment Opportunities* (DOVEO), published by the **Directory of Social Change**, which lists around 500 voluntary organisations most of them offering some sort of volunteer opportunities. Organised into generic types of agencies, such as children, housing/homelessness medicine and overseas, the types of volunteer opportunities outlined include:

- providing administrative support
- fundraising
- being a volunteer visitor
- giving advice
- producing newsletters
- teaching disabled people to ride horses, swim, etc.
- recording various printed materials on tape for blind people
- working in a charity shop
- bereavement counselling
- research
- running friendship clubs

...and so on. The list is almost endless.

> *" CSV will take anyone, whatever your skills or abilities. Your skills are matched with available placements. I originally wanted to go on Voluntary Service Overseas (VSO), but found I was too young. My tutor at college mentioned CSV. CSV sends young people out into the community. You can be placed anywhere in the country. I work on a Young Disabled Unit at a hospital."*
>
> Marie Kerrigan, volunteer with CSV

You may be wondering what particular skills and qualifications you need to become a volunteer. The short answer is none. Anyone of any age and from any background can be a volunteer, even if they are only able to stick stamps on envelopes. We all have some talent or ability we can offer, whether it is standing on a street corner with a tin collecting for say **Help the Aged** or **Christian Aid**, or bringing qualified professional skills as perhaps a solicitor or accountant to assist an organisation's board of trustees. You may be good at organising a charity cricket match or swim-a-thon to raise money, or at keeping an office filing system at peak efficiency. The determining factors are whether the voluntary organisation of your choice needs and welcomes volunteer help, and if so in what capacity. Matching the volunteer's ability with the organisation's needs is the key.

EXAMPLES OF CHARITIES USING VOLUNTEERS

British Trust for Conservation Volunteers (BTCV)

- is Britain's largest practical conservation charity creating opportunities for people to take practical action to protect and improve their environment
- organises numerous projects for protecting the environment, including the rescue of wildlife habitats, management of nature reserves, improvement of access to the countryside and the greening of Britain's towns and cities
- runs over 600 Natural Break and International Conservation Working Holidays and around 500 training courses each year teaching and maintaining practical country-side skills
- works with over 62,000 volunteers each year on a wide range of both urban and rural environmental projects throughout England, Wales & Northern Ireland
- welcomes volunteers from all age groups and backgrounds, and gives them training, support and advice
- offers numerous short-term volunteering opportunities, lasting for a day, a weekend or a week
- also offers longer-term opportunities – three months to a year – to Volunteer Officers, who receive full training and support in many aspects of conservation work, and who often go on to successful careers either with BTCV or other environmental organisations

Citizens Advice Bureau (CAB)

- is the largest generalist advice agency in the country
- deals with a huge range of problems – employment, housing, family, immigration, social security, debt, consumer, education, tax, health and many more, outlined in its leaflet 'Seven Million Questions'
- provides free, confidential and impartial advice
- has a comprehensive national information system, widely acknowledged to be outstanding in its field

- has around thirteen thousand advisers, each trained to nationally agreed standards, 90% of whom are volunteers
- has a detailed training programme
- offers fascinating, rewarding career opportunities

Crisis

- is a national charity
- works to help single homeless people
- runs an Open Christmas shelter every December staffed by volunteers
- has a grant programme for supporting local hostels, day centres and other accommodation schemes all over the country
- provides clean clothing to people who need it through the Crisis Clothing Run
- campaigns to improve long term provision for single homeless people
- uses professional staff and dedicated volunteers to run the organisation.

USEFUL ADDRESSES

Community Service Volunteers, 237 Pentonville Road, London N1 9NJ, tel: 071-278 6601 – runs various programmes including RSVP, the Retired Senior Volunteers Programme

Directory of Social Change, Radius Works, Back Lane, London NW3 1HL, tel: 071-435 8171

The Volunteer Centre UK, 29 Lower King's Road, Berkhamsted, Hertfordshire HP4 2AB, tel: 0442-873311

USEFUL PUBLICATIONS AND OTHER INFORMATION

Organisations such as the **Directory of Social Change** (DSC) and the **Volunteer Centre UK** have various publications to help you understand and find your way around the Voluntary Sector.

The DSC also organises **Charityfair**, an annual event held in the Business Design Centre, London in the spring. It includes many seminars, conferences and workshops to do with a wide range of subjects about the Voluntary Sector, as well as a Volunteering and Employment Forum specifically concerned with paid and unpaid work opportunities.

Understanding Voluntary Organisations, by Charles Handy (published by Penguin, 1990)

The Directory of Volunteer and Employment Opportunities, by Jan Brownfoot and Frances Wilks (published by the Directory of Social Change, 1993)

Third Sector, the news magazine for people in the charity world (published by Art Publishing International)

2
IDENTIFYING THE RIGHT JOB FOR YOU

DECIDING WHICH CAUSES TO WORK FOR

The choice of causes to work for is huge, as we have shown. How do you decide which is the right charity and cause for you? The answer lies in thinking about what you want to do and doing your own research to see what is available. Since every charity has its own 'culture' you must feel committed to the cause <u>and</u> be comfortable with the environment and the people.

To help you decide, ask yourself some preliminary questions:

- which cause or causes are you personally interested in or committed to?
- which voluntary organisations are involved with those causes?
- which offer the right opportunities?
- what type of organisation do *you* want to be involved in?
- how do you contact these organisations?

"I trained as a teacher. I've always worked with children and I've been working as a nanny. I also do voluntary work at a hostel for young mums with babies. I wanted to do something useful. I have an interest in counselling and children, and want to work with children. I'd like to become a counsellor full-time, so I'm doing a training course. I've also joined ChildLine as a volunteer counsellor.**"**

Jo, Volunteer Counsellor, ChildLine

> I joined Action Aid as a volunteer because my family was already involved as sponsors. Action Aid is a development agency. I could identify with its aims and ambitions. I had a desire to contribute and a sense that I could deploy my skills profitably in the social arena and that I should be aiming at doing so. I was also looking for greater breadth and perspective apart from my job, which I have got from being a trustee. Also it's a two-way process. You don't just give, you receive a great amount. What you give to a voluntary organisation you receive back in kind. I have enjoyed every moment of it. The more I put in the more I have received back, and I have been fulfilled by it.

Rodney Buse, Trustee and Chairman of Action Aid/Group Personnel Director, W H Smith

> I joined the voluntary sector because I was in advertising and got fed up with Mammom and the profit motive. I wanted to get back to human values and I wanted to give something back to the community in a meaningful way.

Alarys, Volunteer Counsellor, ChildLine

Once you have made some initial decisions you might then:

- ask friends and relatives who work or volunteer in different charities about what their jobs involve
- ask any charities in which you are seriously interested to send you their annual reports and other information so you can learn more about their work and how they operate. It will be helpful if you enclose a large stamped addressed envelope
- drop by and see what they do, to get a feel for the organisation and its work

> I mentioned to all the organisations and appropriate contacts I knew who worked in the voluntary sector that I was available for voluntary and if possible paid work. I found that there was plenty of opportunity to volunteer and I steered towards those organisations where I had a personal interest or connection. Then I landed a research project job with a branch of Crossroads, which I helped to set up.

Patricia Beecham, Brent Crossroads

Identifying Your Personal Skills and Qualifications

What skills can you offer the voluntary sector? To answer this question you need to give yourself a critical self-appraisal, perhaps with the help of a friend or family member. Do a skills audit on yourself listing all the different kinds of skills and talents that you have with examples of ways in which you have used each. A skill is something you can do or that you have learnt to do, whether through formal education or informally, perhaps through involvement in a club or a hobby. Your skills might range from something very simple, such as being able to collate information in envelopes for mailing out, to something much more advanced such as the ability to organise an event or balance a set of accounts (*see Chapter 4 also*).

Skill	Example of using it
word processing	typing letters, reports
driving	cars, vans
cycling	sponsored cycle ride
cooking	preparing meals for family
child care	looking after own children
DIY	making some shelves
sewing/knitting	making garments
writing	articles for school magazine
organising	church social event
leadership	captain of sports team
fundraising	running a raffle
musical	playing the piano

Apart from practical skills you should also think about what personal qualities you have:

- Are you a caring person, do you enjoy being with people, are you a good listener?
- Are you a motivator, inspiring others?
- Are you well-organised and thorough?
- Are you a good leader?
- Are you a good member of a team?

- Are you an assertive fighter?
- Are you persistent and persuasive?
- Can you cope with pressure? Do you remain cool and calm?
- What do you not enjoy doing?

> *The skills that would be needed for the type of job that I applied for would be administrative, awareness of the voluntary sector, listening skills, empathy and initiative, and an ability to consult with relevant individuals and organisations, and hopefully make the necessary impartial decisions!*
>
> Trisha Ward, Co-ordinator, Holocaust Survivors Centre

You will also need to consider what qualifications you have and what sorts of work they may, or may not, have prepared you for. Did you leave school with any certificates, such as GCSE or A Levels? Have you got any post-school training – a certificate, a diploma, a degree, a National Vocational Qualification (NVQ) or a City & Guilds award? In looking for jobs you may discover that in the voluntary sector it is just not possible to find one that needs precisely your particular skill or qualification. You may have to think imaginatively about the sort of job you can, or would like, to do, in which perhaps you can use the skills that the qualification has given you

> *I have a BSc in Genetics and an MSc in Human Genetics. I also worked as a financial trader for three years. This gave me good corporate experience which is an excellent foundation for corporate and other fundraising.*
>
> Sheenagh Day, Fundraising Manager, Family Planning Association (FPA)

> *I did Physics with Philosophy at university because Physics was the easiest subject for me to do. I liked English and writing too, and I was interested in transport issues. Now as a volunteer at Transport 2000 I'm working on the magazine and in desk top publishing. It's a long way from Physics, but I'm enjoying it. I've learnt a lot and taught myself a lot and I feel I'm doing something useful.*
>
> Barney Stringer, volunteer with Transport 2000

rather than specific subject knowledge. Some people who have degrees in, for example, science subjects have got jobs in voluntary organisations in fundraising and desk top publishing.

Once you have assessed your various talents and abilities, you will need to decide whether you want to use your existing skills or whether you would prefer to learn and develop new ones. What kind of work do you want to do? What do you feel you can best do? Once you have decided what appeals most, you will then need to find out whether such skills are required.

> **"** I left my job as a Chartered Accountant in January 1992 and joined the Working for a Charity [WFAC] course to gain an insight into the voluntary sector. I did my placement at the Royal Marsden Cancer Appeal and continued there part-time until I got my present job. I also approached my local Volunteer Bureau to offer my services and became Honorary Treasurer for two Councils for Voluntary Service. Through these experiences I decided that I definitely wanted to get paid employment in the voluntary sector. My current job was advertised in The Guardian. The person specification said qualified or part-qualified accountant essential and experience of the voluntary sector desirable. The advantages are that it involves a wider variety of things than would be possible if I were just doing accountancy work and I have learnt a lot of new skills. **"**
> Elise McGreevy, Head of Finance & Administration, Crisis

> **"** I think you need to be a self-starter, self motivated and self sufficient to work in the voluntary sector. It also helps to be computer literate and to have a basic business sense. **"**
> Sheenagh Day, Fundraising Manager, Family Planning Association

> **"** I really do think that the only necessary skills needed to be a volunteer are open-mindedness, enthusiasm and commitment. By supplying these, the rewards are vast: it is quite simply a case of 'getting out whatever you put in'. **"**
> Janet Bell, volunteer with Community Service Volunteers (CSV)

Deciding the Sort of Job you might do

What skills are relevant to the voluntary sector? You need to ask yourself what skills do charities want and what skills do you have to offer? You will need to do some more research to answer these questions for your own circumstances, since the sector as a whole uses as wide a range of professional and other skills as do the private and public sectors. Voluntary organisations need people with organisational, research, practical, analytical, administrative and inter-personal skills, among others.

The Types of Job Available

The following list is just a selection of the many jobs available:
- financial (e.g. accountants, book-keeping)
- personnel work
- computer operators/database programmers
- administration and management (of the organisation) (e.g. directors, office managers)
- office administration and clerical (e.g. secretaries, clerks, receptionists)
- public relations (e.g. press officers, publications officers, lobbyists)
- communication and publications (e.g. writing and editing)
- design and desk-top publishing
- fundraising (e.g. corporate fundraising, special events organisers, direct mail specialists, trading officers, community fundraisers, etc.)
- care staff (e.g. housing workers, counsellors, social workers)

Once again ask friends and relations involved in the voluntary sector to let you know if they hear of any jobs, and for their suggestions about where your skills might be appropriate. Read through literature from your shortlist of charities that you feel are right for you to find out about the kinds of positions they need to fill. Look also at charity jobs advertisements. This will give you a good idea of the sorts of abilities and experience which are being asked for.

The voluntary sector today is becoming increasingly professional, and many charities are able to offer appropriate career structures for people who have the right skills and interest. You will find it easier to 'get in' if you have prior work experience, but experience as a volunteer can also count.

Voluntary organisations are also looking for certain personal qualities. Commitment, enthusiasm, patience and flexibility are all valued. So is reliability. Since working in the voluntary sector often means working long hours in somewhat unstructured conditions, for less money than the salaries in other sectors, you need to be dedicated and committed to the organisation's mission and aims.

> *" Even though the financial remuneration may be less than in the private sector, there is considerable satisfaction and fulfilment in working to help to better other peoples' lives – and it is nice to be 'needed'! The work can also be considerably more varied and challenging."*
> Patricia Beecham, Brent Crossroads

Equally as important as the voluntary sector's needs for the right employees and volunteers, are your needs for yourself. It is important to be very clear about why you want to work for a charity. In what ways do you think it is going to be different, and perhaps better, than working for any other kind of organisation? What do you hope to get out of it? It is also important to realise that working in the voluntary sector is not an easy option. The demands can be very heavy and there may be many frustrations, especially if finances are limited.

In seeking a position in a voluntary organisation ask yourself:

- How much **responsibility** do you want?
- Are you interested in **management** or would you rather be managed? Do you want to be in the front line or are you happy to keep in the background? Perhaps you would rather begin in a less high profile role but have the opportunities for promotion and advancement to a more senior level
- Do you fully share the organisation's **aims** and **ethos**?
- Are you able to **cope with people** making demands on you when you know that you will not be able to fully solve their problems?
- Do you want to be doing the **caring** or working in an **office**?
- What **motivates** you – using your skills, helping others, doing a job well, enjoying what you do, gaining personal fulfilment?

- How important is the size of your **salary** to you?
- Are you willing to begin as a **volunteer** and perhaps move on to paid work?

Your answers to these questions will help you determine the sort of job you want to do in the voluntary sector and the level at which you would like to start.

> *I wrote to Community Service Volunteers (CSV) for information. There followed an informal chat with a Volunteer Director. This gave both her and myself the chance to discuss the options available to me. I soon realised that there was a vast range of work to choose from. My placement is with a residential home for mentally and physically frail older people. This is an area of work that I had not previously considered, but nevertheless have thoroughly enjoyed. My role within the home is to provide a number of activities for the members to join in. I took the borough's driving test so that I could drive the ambulance. This has increased the range of activities possible.*

Janet Bell, volunteer with CSV

> *The advice I would give is, if you are really keen on the job, mug up on your subject thoroughly. Even get a friend to do a dummy interview and role play. But mug up, mug up, mug up.*

Trisha Ward, Co-ordinator, Holocaust Survivors Centre

When you see a position which you feel might suit you, you will then need to get details about it and fill in any necessary application forms, write your CV for the requirements of the job and so on. Since there is likely to be much competition for it, decide how much you really want the job.

Alternatively, you might decide after doing you research and seeing what is available, that you would prefer to create your own job and start your own organisation/charity. Tory Laughland, Editor/ Director of Who Cares, a magazine for young people in care, did just that. In 1992, after some years in existence, the magazine project became a charity with the objects of furthering the well-being of children in care and developing a programme of action. (*See also Chapter 13 on Setting Up Your Own Organisation*)

> *"My expectations have been wildly exceeded; my learning curve has been a vertical line. I've had to learn about management, training, forward planning, personnel, finances. The way through has been to get really good advisors, some paid and some on a voluntary basis. The thrill for me is the prospect of structural change...in the care system in Britain."*
> Tory Laughland, Editor/Director, Who Cares

IDENTIFYING YOUR OWN REQUIREMENTS

Before contacting an organisation about a paid or voluntary job, think about your own practical requirements and whether there are any special needs or limitations which you must take into account:

- **Where** do you want to work – must it be near home or are you prepared to travel. If you don't mind travelling, how far away are you willing to go and how long can you spend getting there?
- **How much time** can you give, if volunteering, or if you want paid work, must this be full-time or could it be part-time?
- Can you work **any day** of the week and any time of day, or can you only manage certain days and times? Are you available during school holidays?
- Do you want a **regular commitment** or to be called upon when needed?
- Do you have any **special needs** (e.g. must you sit down to work)? Do you have any disabilities that may require special facilities?
- Are there any particular **limitations** on your working (e.g. you receive welfare benefits, or are undertaking a training course)?

> *"There are many voluntary organisations which can only afford to employ part-timers, which suits my lifestyle. I had to look for work that would suit my lifestyle, accommodate the needs of my children – perhaps letting me work longer hours during the school term and taking more time off during the holidays. I have been extremely fortunate to find a job that is five minutes drive away. However, the child care I need does take up about half my income!"*
> Trisha Ward, Co-ordinator, Holocaust Survivors Centre

> **"** I originally wanted to do Voluntary Service Overseas (VSO), but found I was too young. My tutor at college mentioned Community Service Volunteers (CSV) which sends people out into the community. You can be placed anywhere in the country. You receive free lodging, pocket money and food allowance. This was ideal for me. Also I really didn't mind what kind of work I got, so I was placed in three months. **"**
>
> Marie Kerrigan, volunteer with CSV

USEFUL PUBLICATIONS AND OTHER INFORMATION

The Volunteer Centre UK, 29 Lower King's Road, Berkhamsted, Hertfordshire HP4 2AB, tel: 0442-873311 has various publications and leaflets available about working and volunteering in the voluntary sector. They include:
Do It! Volunteer Now, 1993 in conjunction with the BBC

Directory of Social Change, Radius Works, Back Lane, London NW3 1HL, tel: 071-435 8171 also has a number of useful, relevant publications, including:
The Directory of Volunteer and Employment Opportunities by Jan Brownfoot and Frances Wilks, 1993

Other useful publications include:

The Voluntary Agencies Directory, National Council for Voluntary Organisations (Bedford Square Press) 1992

Volunteer Work, by Hilary Sewell, Central Bureau for Educational Visits and Exchanges, 1988

Third Sector, the news magazine for people in the charity world, published by Art Publishing International

3
BECOMING A VOLUNTEER

> *If you want to go into voluntary work, decide what you want to do. Look at your abilities, what service you can offer and your skills. Look for organisations who need those skills. Look at the job and try to match your skills. If you haven't got them all – find training and people to support you. Decide what you want to do and go for it!*
>
> John Kelly, volunteer, Surrey PHAB (Physically Handicapped and Able-Bodied)

BECOMING A VOLUNTEER

Some 23 million people volunteer every year. Many people you come into contact with in everyday life are volunteers. They:

- raise funds
- answer telephone helplines
- are hospital drivers
- teach skills
- organise sports clubs
- conserve the environment
- work in charity shops
- serve as trustees and on management committees
- start charities and self-help groups

to name but a few activities that volunteers are involved in.

Many charities and self-help groups are run partly or entirely by volunteers. Volunteers are involved not only in the voluntary sector but also in the statutory sector (e.g. in hospitals and schools). Some volunteers give a few hours a week or a few days per year, while others give much of their time. Sometimes the only significant difference between a volunteer and a paid employee is that the employee receives a salary. Although volunteers give their time for nothing, the jobs they do are just as important and require just as much skill as any equivalent paid position.

People volunteer from all ages and walks of life and for a wide variety of reasons. A young person may volunteer to get experience of a particular kind of job or of life in general. An older person may volunteer to learn a different set of skills or to meet new people or to have something fulfilling to do after retirement or during a spell of unemployment. It is important to recognise why you want to volunteer and know what you have to offer before you set about looking for the right opportunity.

What do Volunteers do?

You can do an enormous range of things as a volunteer. Here are just a few examples of what voluntary organisations can need:

- Administrative assistance
- Advice giving
- Answering the telephone
- Auditing/Book-keeping
- Befriending
- Car maintenance
- Computer skills
- Counselling
- Disability awareness training
- Dog walking
- Driving/Escorting
- First Aid
- Fundraising
- Helping to run a stall/ coffee bar
- Gardening
- Holiday hosting
- Lobbying/campaigning
- Management Committee membership
- Painting and decorating
- Play scheme
- Press/PR
- Public speaking
- Running a self-help group
- Sailing
- School Governing
- Trustees
- Youth work

> **If volunteering is something that a person wants to do, I believe that they should go for it. They should try volunteering no matter what their age, sex, skin colour. There are so many people out there with something to give and maybe it's only their lack of confidence which is stopping them. This includes people who've had problems with drugs or alcohol and have been on recovery projects for these. They shouldn't be afraid to get involved either because they can use the knowledge and experience they've gained.**
>
> Carol, volunteer counsellor, ChildLine

> **I don't want to enter full-time employment – there are too many exciting opportunities opening up right now as a volunteer.**
>
> John Kelly, volunteer, Surrey PHAB (Physically Handicapped and Able-Bodied)

This is not an exhaustive list by any means. You may want to look at the section at the end of the book on *"Assessing Your Skills and Attributes"* for more information. When you have discovered what you can do and would like to offer, then set about finding a charity who could use your skills. For example, if you have a dog and you enjoy walking it, then you are an experienced dog walker and could perhaps walk an elderly or disabled person's dog. (There are a number of places you can research the right charity for you – details are in the section on *"Finding out what's available"*).

WHAT DO YOU WANT FROM VOLUNTEERING?

You may want to volunteer for personal or career reasons or a mixture of both. Personal reasons could include:

- feeling strongly about a charity's cause and wanting to do something to help
- having a 'gap' year to fill before going to college or university
- a friend, who is a volunteer, asking you for your help
- having time available on a regular basis and wanting to do something useful
- wanting to meet new friends.

> **I had chosen to take redundancy because I wanted to have a holiday and take time to think. But you can get very lonely and there is loss of community, too. For me, volunteering means working with and for others, and it keeps up my self-esteem.**
>
> Malcolm, volunteer counsellor, ChildLine

If you are thinking in terms of developing your career your reasons might include:

- wanting to learn a new skill
- trying to improve your employment prospects and add to your CV (Curriculum Vitae)
- needing specific experience before applying for a training course
- thinking that you might like to work in the voluntary sector but wanting to check it out first.

> **I've loved volunteering for Victim Support and it's had a tremendous impact on my life in terms of direction and a change of career. I'm going to start a new job with Newham Action Against Domestic Violence. I started there as a volunteer, too, and now I've got a post as funding has recently come through. I feel a real sense of achievement.**
>
> Sarah, volunteer, Victim Support

Once you have identified your reasons for volunteering, the next step is to make your own checklist of questions you would ask any potential charity. They could include some of the following:

- What are the aims and objectives of the organisation?
- Will I work alone or with others?
- Can I work with you for the whole period of my 'gap' year?
- Are training and support provided?
- Will this experience help me in my future career?

What have you got to offer a Voluntary Organisation?

Before making contact with an organisation, think about what you are able to offer them. Ask yourself:

- How much time can I give?
- Can I offer a regular commitment, or a few hours at short notice when there's a crisis?
- What skills am I able to offer?
- What special interests/knowledge do I have?
- What personal qualities do I possess?
- What am I physically able to do?
- Do I need any special facilities or support?

" At the end of the day I want to do the best for the organisation I work for – it's a bonus if I get something out of it."
John Kelly, volunteer, Surrey PHAB (Physically Handicapped and Able-Bodied)

" As an air stewardess I get blocks of days off. I wasn't putting them to much use. I wanted to help other people, to be in touch with them on a one-to-one basis, say befriending. But because of the shift patterns of my professional work, it's very difficult to fit in anything on-going and regular. So I went to my local Volunteer Bureau and said 'can I be of use to anyone?' they said 'yes' and suggested counselling preceded by training. Now I squeeze in counselling for ChildLine around my shifts. Sometimes I go home shattered but I couldn't give it up."
Karen, volunteer counsellor, ChildLine

Finding out what's available

Organisations that involve volunteers range right across the spectrum of voluntary and statutory organisations. There are various routes to find out what's on offer.

Signposts is a national database containing information about local volunteering opportunities. Contact **The Volunteer Centre UK** (*address at end of chapter*) if you would like a search undertaken in your area.

Volunteer Bureaux act as volunteering 'job shops'. They have a range of information about local opportunities and contacts and can offer advice.

Councils for Voluntary Service (CVS): the name may vary locally so look in your phone book or Yellow Pages under 'volunteers' or 'voluntary'. CVS are in touch with most of the larger local organisations and projects that involve volunteers. In rural areas they are called **Rural Community Councils**.

Local radio and press may have special spots or regular features about voluntary work.

Adult Education Centres may organise general introductory course which provide a good introduction for volunteers or training for specific sorts of work.

Public Libraries usually have information and often posters about volunteer opportunities.

"*Directory of Volunteer and Employment Opportunities*" (published by the Directory of Social Change) lists a variety of voluntary and charitable organisations, including self-help groups, which involve volunteers.

Museums, nature reserves and parks often have information about environmental groups and opportunities.

Make use of your local networks and ask friends, relatives, or colleagues about their experiences of volunteering.

If you have 'Teletext', opportunities for volunteers around the country are broadcast at weekends on Ceefax on page 486.

> **"** *I found out about becoming a Community Service Volunteer (CSV) initially through meeting another person who was volunteering as a CSV. I found the address to write to in my local careers library and sent off for information.* **"**
> Janet Bell, a CSV (Community Service Volunteer)

MAKING CONTACT

When you have found an organisation which interests you, either telephone or write them a letter. If you decide to write, a preliminary phone call can identify the person to write to.

If you phone, explain clearly that you want to volunteer. Different charities have different job titles for the person responsible for volunteers. Charities who involve large numbers of volunteers may have a volunteer co-ordinator. If there is no one person with the specific responsibility for volunteers, as to speak to the Personnel Department or, in smaller charities, the Director.

If you write:

- indicate your interest
- be as specific as you can about what you want to do and what you have to offer
- ask for some information about the organisation, such as the Annual Report or an explanatory leaflet
- suggest an informal meeting.

You may then be asked to fill in an application form. Some organisations ask for references, too. Organisations working with vulnerable people and children usually have to get police screening for both paid and voluntary staff.

> **"** My advice to anyone thinking of becoming a volunteer would be – take on a bit at a time and see how you go. The most important thing for any volunteer is to learn to say no clearly. **"**
>
> Sarah, volunteer, Victim Support

Negotiating Terms and Conditions

Once you have been accepted into an organisation you will need to be very clear about your involvement. You should

- ask for a job description setting out what you are expected to do
- check the hours and times you will be expected to work
- make sure you know who will be responsible for giving you support and guidance
- ask whether there is an induction procedure to enable you to get to know the organisation, the staff and the work
- satisfy yourself that Health and Safety regulations are being adhered to
- enquire what training will be available, and what opportunities there may be for development
- find out whether your travel and out-of-pocket expenses will be paid
- ask if there is a volunteer allowance.

Be aware of your own personal boundaries and limits. Don't take on too much otherwise you may run the risk of 'burning-out'. Agree to something that you can do. Say no if you are asked to take on something you can't do.

REMUNERATION AND EXPENSES

Some voluntary agencies can pay their full-time volunteers a volunteer allowance. Although this is not a salary, it can be a considerable help especially if the volunteer is on a fixed or low income or a pension.

There may be out-of-pocket expenses connected with volunteering e.g. fares, food, phone calls, protective clothing. People may not be able to volunteer unless these are reimbursed. Many organisations have a clear policy on this. It is important that organisations offer to reimburse out-of-pocket expenses as a matter of course as this ensures that volunteering is available to everyone. This is also part of having an Equal Opportunities policy.

" I work as a Community Service volunteer on a Disabled Unit in a hospital. I feel good about what I am doing. The sense of satisfaction I get when helping to rehabilitate a client, and you've been struggling, and suddenly it all comes together. There's nothing to march it. It's also very tough and frustrating, especially when you have a terminally ill client. But one advantage I have as a volunteer over a trained person is that I have time to make friends with the clients, which is a very big plus.

I also get an enormous amount of support, not only from CSV but also from my placement. I work with my supervisor on the Disabled Unit. When I arrived I had supervised sessions for the first three weeks. We discussed what I had been doing, how I was feeling and any problems I'd had. I found it a great help."

Marie Kerrigan, a CSV (Community Service Volunteer)

Some charities don't pay, or don't offer to pay volunteers expenses. This may be because they can't afford to, or because they can attract volunteers who don't need or want to claim. Organisations which genuinely can't afford to pay expenses should make this clear from the start.

The Inland Revenue and DSS (Department of Social Security) have various regulations regarding legitimate and reasonable expenses, including those for volunteer drivers. There are also regulations for when volunteer payments become 'earnings' and affect income support benefits.

For further details, see the Volunteer Centre UK booklet *"All Expenses Paid"* by Angela Whitcher.

Training and Support

Training of some kind is necessary for most volunteer roles. It can vary from a pre-volunteering course of some weeks' or months' duration (especially when you may need special skills for counselling or advice-giving) to an informal induction.

> **"** The CAB (Citizens Advice Bureau) trains a wide cross-section of advisers, including young people, the unemployed and those from ethnic minorities. There are about 1,300 bureaux in the country. 90% of the workforce is voluntary and they, like the 10% of paid workers are all trained to the same standard and expected to give the same level of expertise. **"**
> Joan Price, volunteer worker, CAB

> **"** We have all sorts of volunteers – at the Project, advice givers, at the Housing Trust, fundraisers and interior decorators. Bunches of old ladies make curtains. I have found that volunteers need a lot of support and encouragement. You need to put a lot of care into setting things up properly. **"**
> Gill Fitzhugh, the Portobello Project

As well as training you should receive on-going support. Most organisations do provide some support for their volunteers. This can take the form of regular supervision or having someone to talk to on an informal basis or on-the-job short course (training which includes helping you understand the role of the organisation and the role you will play).

Organising other Volunteers

You may be in a position that requires you to organise other volunteers. Tigger Hewitt, a volunteer organiser for RSVP, the Community Service Volunteers Senior volunteering programme, has summed up her advice arising from her experience.

1 Be open to all possibilities
2 Be open-minded – but be careful in your judgement.

Sometimes one can co-opt the most unlikely people

3 Make sure the potential volunteer knows what the job entails

4 Keep in touch regularly

5 Be appreciative – always thank your volunteers – cards, messages, even flowers when appropriate

6 Offer expenses – petrol money, bus fares, phone calls

7 Make sure volunteers are covered by insurance and that they know this

8 Be available to support and to stand in if necessary

9 Be not proud – apologise if you make a mistake

10 Have a good Treasurer and Secretary

11 Be on good terms with the press – keep them informed and write them a 'thank you' letter if they do a good article

12 Give yourself plenty of 'breathing space'

THE VOLUNTEERS CHARTER

Tigger Hewitt, Volunteer Organiser for the RSVP senior volunteering programme, passes on the benefit of her experience as a volunteer in her version of a Volunteers Charter.

1 Make sure you really want to volunteer

2 Only volunteer if you are prepared to do the job regularly (give or take holidays and illness)

3 Give yourself time to think of your commitments, your strengths, your energies

4 Have the courage to try something different – you may be very happy doing something you thought you couldn't manage

5 Do what you enjoy

6 Smile and enjoy what you're doing

7 Learn to say 'no' gracefully but firmly

8 Make sure you want to say 'yes'

9 Don't expect thanks – but it's nice when you get them!

10 If it all gets too much – don't try to struggle on. Give notice that you are leaving and stop. Or – change the area or kind of work you do.

Finally – ENJOY VOLUNTEERING

Good luck!

FURTHER INFORMATION

The **Volunteer Centre UK**, 29 Lower King's Road, Berkhamsted, Herts HP24 2AB, tel: 0442-873311, produces the following:

- **'Voluntary Opportunities in the UK'**, Information sheet, £1
- **'Voluntary Opportunities Overseas'**, Information sheet, £1
- **'Volunteer, Welfare Benefits and Taxation'**, Information sheet, £1
- **'So you want to be a volunteer?'**, Resource pack, £4
- **'Volunteers First: a guideline to the personnel responsibilities of people who manage volunteers'**, £1.50.
- **'All Expenses Paid'**, Booklet by Angela Whitcher

The **Directory of Social Change**, Radius Works, Back Lane, London NW3 1HL, tel: 071-435 8171, publishes many books on the voluntary sector, including a *'Directory of Volunteer and Employment Opportunities'*.

4
SETTING ABOUT GETTING PAID EMPLOYMENT

The voluntary sector provides challenging and rewarding career opportunities. Working for a charity is no longer seen as a low paid job for the worthy or as a second-best career option or as something to do after early retirement or because other options are closed to you. Some people choose to make their careers in the voluntary sector. Others enter the voluntary sector after working elsewhere as a positive career choice, bringing valuable experience and professional skills.

> " I began work in the Citizens Advice Bureau (CAB) as a volunteer adviser and went on to paid work as a manager. Others, begin their careers at the very start, as paid advisers or as paid managers, or as paid admin workers. Others, who may have joined as volunteers, become paid employees and join the staff at our national and area offices. Yet others work as paid CAB advisers in a variety of CAB projects or outreach sessions held in such places as prisons and hospitals. "
>
> Joan Price, CAB (Citizens Advice Bureau) worker

Job hunting in the voluntary sector varies from individual to individual, but there are some general guidelines. These are not hard and fast rules – just the benefits of other peoples' experience.

There are various ways of seeking employment in voluntary organisations. Many people find it useful to structure their job hunting into a Job Search Campaign.

Starting a Job Search Campaign

If you are thinking about paid employment, there is one big issue to take on board. That is the fact that there are around 3 million unemployed people looking for work. Except where very specialist skills which are in short supply are needed, there are likely to be many hundreds of people applying for each job or approaching organisations asking about the possibilities of employment. This means that you will have to work hard at the business of getting a job.

> **"** My advice to anyone thinking of working in the voluntary sector is contained in one word – persevere. If you are interested keep going until you succeed. **"**
> Sheenagh Day, Fundraising Manager, Family Planning Association

Another point to bear in mind is that many organisations have an Equal Opportunities policy. This inevitably means that they have formal procedures for advertising jobs and for the selection process. Even if you want to work for a particular organisation, there has to be a job available and you have to be selected. However, you can start by volunteering, and a volunteer is often in a good position to be considered for employment if and when a job vacancy occurs. Knowledge of the organisation and its work, a recognition of the contribution already made and the skills brought to the job, and good personal relationships are all in your favour.

When starting a job search campaign, you need to bear in mind the importance of:

- spending time to research and identify the right charity
- good presentation – this can make your application stand out from hundreds of others
- managing your job search campaign to leave you time for leisure (and for volunteering!)
- finding a friend who is also looking for work and offering each other mutual encouragement and support. This process is often called 'buddying'.

THE RIGHT ORGANISATION FOR YOU

As already noted, each charity has its own 'culture' or style of operating. As well as being committed to an organisation's cause, it is important that you feel comfortable in it. You may already have asked yourself the following questions, but if you haven't, it is important to do so now:

- Which causes are you committed to?
- Which jobs would use your current skills and experience?
- Which charities might offer you the right work opportunities?

You might find it helpful to:

- do voluntary work for a charity whose aims you support
- speak to friends who work or volunteer in different charities about their jobs
- ask a charity to send you a copy of its Annual Report to find out more about its work.

Looking at your Skills

Look at the skills you can offer. Be realistic about what you can't do, too. Your skills may be obvious, e.g. secretarial or accountancy. Or they may be less obvious and you may not even recognise them yourself. You may want to consult the section on *"Assessing Your Skills and Attributes"* at the end of the book.

> **“** I did a ten week course at Hatfield Polytechnic (now the University of Hertfordshire) called New Opportunities for Women. We did various skills practices including a video taped interview. I realised that I sat like a sack of potatoes and kept saying 'ummmmm'. So the advice I would give is: get a friend do a dummy interview with you and a role play. If you can be videoed, this is invaluable. **”**
>
> *Patricia Beecham, Brent Crossroads*

You probably have more skills and more relevant experience than you think. It is a matter of seeing what these are and explaining them effectively. If you are returning to work after a long break or coping with redundancy, confidence can be a problem. This can be overcome by having a 'buddy' in a similar position to you. Arrange to spend time together on a regular basis working on getting a job. List the other person's skills and practice interviews together. Set yourself attainable goals each day and keep to them.

You may decide you don't have all the skills you need. Two major ways of acquiring them are: training and volunteering or a combination of both. The benefits are:

- volunteering gives you relevant hands-on experience of the voluntary sector. (*See Chapter 3 for more details*).
- training gives you specific skills and an overview into which to fit your experience. Many training courses that are now being run include a volunteer placement element.

Training Courses

Working for a Charity, 44-46 Caversham Road, London NW5 2DS, tel: 071-911 0353 (charity administration, marketing and fundraising information and a ten week placement).

Institute of Charity Fundraising Managers, 208 Market Towers, 1 Nine Elms Lane, London SW8 5NQ, tel: 071-627 3436 (a four-day basic fundraising course).

DIFFERENT APPROACHES TO THE CHARITY

There are four main approaches to getting a job in a charity or voluntary organisation. They are:

- writing in
- applying to ads
- approaching specialist recruitment agencies
- networking.

Writing in

Writing speculative letters to a large number of organisations is probably the hardest way of getting a job, but some people do succeed. If your letter hits the right desk at the right moment, you may be lucky. However, it is also worth bearing in mind that many voluntary organisations have equal opportunities policies. This means they must go through formal selection processes before they appoint anyone. This usually involves advertising the post.

If you try the speculative letter approach, remember to:

- telephone the charity and ask who to address the letter to
- look up relevant details about the charity in a directory or a handbook so you can personalise each letter
- include a succinct CV (Curriculum Vitae) highlighting the main achievements of your career.

Applying to Ads

Many jobs in the sector are advertised in the press. The key places to look are:

- The Guardian (Mondays for Marketing, Fundraising and PR and Wednesdays for voluntary sector jobs in general)
- The Independent on Thursdays
- The Sunday Times (for more senior appointments)
- Local newspapers
- Specialist journals such as Community Care, Social Work, Nursing Times (for caring jobs)
- Publications such as The Voice, The Caribbean Times, The Asian Times
- Charity newsletters (where they advertise their own jobs).

When you have found an advertisement that interests you, read it carefully again and consider the following:

- Do you have all or most of the skills, personal qualities and experience they are asking for?
- If there are one or two specified skills which you don't yet possess – can you demonstrate an ability to acquire them speedily?
- Is it an organisation whose aims you are in sympathy with?

Be prepared to adjust your CV for the advertisement so that you highlight the things they are looking for. If an application form is required, you may also want to attach your CV. (*See the section on CVs and Application Forms for tips*). Write a brief covering letter outlining your skills and your interest in the organisation.

You should bear in mind that the many jobs ads attract hundreds of replies. So unless you have very relevant skills or experience that you can demonstrate clearly, your chances of getting shortlisted are quite slim.

> Replying to advertisements is not the only way of trying to get a job. Think about some of the other things you can do.

Specialist Recruitment Agencies

Recruitment consultants are retained by charities and voluntary organisations to help them find appropriate staff. Often the consultants will advertise on the organisation's behalf, select and interview applicants, and put a short list through to the Personnel Manager.

The same basic guidelines apply. Make sure you provide:

- a good **CV** or well-filled in **application form**
- a clear and brief **covering letter** showing evidence of ability to do the job as well as clear motivation.

There are three main recruitment agencies for the voluntary sector:

CR Charity Recruitment, 40 Rosebery Avenue, London EC1R 4RN, tel: 071-833 0770

Charity People, Suite 308, The Chandlery, 50 Westminster Bridge Road, London SE1 7QY, tel: 071-721 7585

Charity Appointments, 3 Spitals Yard, London E1 6AQ, tel: 071-247 4502.

Networking

There are two forms of networking:

- **group networking** – a group of individuals who discuss issues and problems, share information and provide each other with support
- **professional networking** – a way of increasing your professional contacts and hearing about opportunities

Group Networking

This is a group of people getting together regularly to share information on an informal basis. Often the group will meet in someone's house, local centre or Jobclub. You may hear about it through friends or contacts or, if you already have a 'buddy', you might set one up and ask a few others to join you.

The benefits are:

- you can give each other support and encouragement
- you can pool ideas, knowledge and resources

>You can approach a recruitment agency direct, sending your CV, stating your career intentions and highlighting your special skills.

- if a person knows of a job for which they are not suitable, they can pass it on to someone else in the group.

The Working for a Charity course encourages participants to network with each other on the course and to keep in touch afterwards. The **Charity Forum**, which is a national membership organisation for people working in marketing and fundraising, arranges a lunchtime talk once a month in London which provides opportunities to meet other people working in the sector.

Professional Networking

This is the process by which personal contacts are used to assist you in your job search. It is not about asking people you know for a job. It is about getting information which will help you get a job. For example, you may:

- hear about opportunities before they are advertised
- get interesting information which you can use at an interview
- increase your confidence and practise your interview skills
- get good feedback on your CV.

Very often, when people say they were in the right place at the right time, they have been networking, either consciously or not. Networking maximises your chances of being in the right place at the right time.

Networking can be particularly effective when you are changing careers after redundancy or a career break as you have established skills to offer. If you are currently unemployed, networking is a good way of getting your confidence back.

The first thing to do is to list all the people you know who may be able to help you. They could include:

- anyone who works, or has worked, in the voluntary sector
- anyone who works in sectors which serve the voluntary sector
- anyone who does voluntary work for a charity.

You may not feel confident to approach all the people you have listed so start with the ones you feel are most friendly and willing to assist you.

Getting in Touch

There are several ways to get in touch with your contacts:

- write a letter
- telephone
- ask someone else to arrange the meeting.

Writing a Networking Letter

The objective of the letter is to obtain a meeting not a job. Try to come across as positive and relaxed. To give this impression, every letter should:

- have a confident story. You may be unemployed right now, but if you come across as calm and relaxed about it, people will accept that. After all most of us have gone through the experience in some form or another at some time. Give an account of your circumstances which sounds positive and hopeful.

- include a reason why you want to see him or her. A little bit of flattery can go a long way here! For example, you might say: 'It occurred to me that you have an excellent grasp of fundraising gained in a variety of voluntary organisations.'

- say what you want. Stress the fact that you want information. You might say something: 'I wondered if you could spare half an hour of your time to discuss the possibilities?'

- suggest a follow-up activity. Tell them you will phone in a few days to see if a meeting is possible. Make sure you do this.

Don't send a CV unless you feel the circumstances particularly warrant it.

Tips for Phoning

- If you haven't got access to a phone, buy a phone card and choose a quiet location.

- Try calling early in the morning e.g. 8.30 am. Busy people are often in the office then and it shows you are up and about.

- Stand up – it can make your voice sound more positive than if you are sitting on your bed. Remember to speak clearly and at your normal speed.

- Practice what you are going to say by role-playing the call with a friend.
- If the secretary answers the phone, imply that the call is personal.

If you know people rather better, you may be able to phone them directly and suggest a meeting. If you have friends who are able to help you, ask them to arrange the meeting.

> **"** *At the outset I wrote a standard letter with varying introductions to over a hundred contacts explaining that I was thinking of working in the voluntary sector and seeking their advice. These letters bore fruit. I had meetings and received introductions. In this way I learned more about the voluntary sector and was able to define in which area I wanted to work. I wrote notes on what I had learned from these experiences.*
>
> *I realised through this process that I wanted to work for an organisation that uses business skills and knowledge to help solve community problems. I went to Business in the Community (BITC) on a 20 day work placement as part of the Working for a Charity course. I used this period to make numerous contacts both within the organisation and with those connected with it in some way. I requested a meeting with the Chief Executive and learnt later that he was setting up a new organisation London First. Later that year I sought a further meeting with him 'for advice' and he invited me to join London First. We agreed that I would work on a voluntary basis for four weeks to test compatibility. After that it was a mutual decision for me to join on an employed basis.* **"**
>
> Pam, London First.

At the Meeting

You are after information, tips and suggestions of all sorts. Prepare a list of questions. The sorts of questions you ask will vary with your circumstances but here are a few possible approaches. Adapt them to suit yourself:

- Having just left college, where I enjoyed being a volunteer, I am thinking about a career in the voluntary sector. What advice could you give me?

- I am thinking of changing the direction of my career – having been in marketing for the last ten years. Can you suggest I how I could enhance my skills to interest a charity?
- I've got a background in finance and administration – how can I transfer across to the charity sector?
- I'm planning to return to work after bringing up my children. I'd like to use my secretarial skills and find some meaningful work. How would you go about it?
- Now I'm in my fifties and with changing family commitments, I don't need to earn so much money. I'd really like to work for a charity – in what ways do you think my skills and experience could be valuable?
- I'm trying to make the transition from voluntary to paid work – are there any suggestions you could make?
- Can you suggest anyone else I might be able to go and see?

One aim of the meeting should be, if possible, to obtain another contact who you can then write to using the first contact's name. Repeat the procedure with as many contacts as you are given.

Networking takes time and effort but it can be an effective way of getting a job.

CVs, Accompanying Letters and Application Forms

CVs

You may like to turn to Appendix 2 at the back of the book, *How to write a Successful CV* for more detailed advice.

The aim of your CV is to get you an interview. It is your primary marketing tool and, apart from the accompanying letter or application form, will be all an organisation will know about you. It should describe the best of you – the unique experience that has gone to make up your life.

The basic points to bear in mind are:
- a CV should not exceed two sides of typed A4 paper
- personal details e.g. name, address, date of birth etc. should appear at the beginning

- latest experience should appear first
- give information about each job or life experience, preferably in bullet point form about what you have achieved. (*See Appendix 1, Assessing Your skills and Attributes, for help with this*)
- hobbies/interests and any referees should appear at the end of a CV.

> Your CV is your primary marketing tool. Make sure it is as good as you can make it.

Accompanying Letters

Letters should be no longer than one side of typed A4 paper. Each should contain:

- a statement about the job you're applying for and how you heard about the vacancy
- a brief summary of your qualifications and experience including any voluntary work
- a short section linking your skills to the needs of the job. Show in a confident, specific way that you could do the job.
- a final paragraph, re-stating your interest in the job and anticipating the possibility of a meeting.

Presentation is important. Make sure you:

- use plain white A4 paper and standard business envelopes
- address the letter correctly. If necessary call the organisation beforehand to check the correct person to address the letter to and check the spelling of their name
- write short sentences which are as natural and jargon-free as possible
- check the spelling of your letter and your CV.

Application Forms

Because of the move towards equal opportunities organisations are tending to use application forms more and more. The following basic guidelines may help your to stand out from the crowd:

- take a photocopy of the form and practice with it first
- type the form if possible, otherwise hand write it neatly
- read the 'person specification' and cover each requirement with examples from your own experience

- forms often have too little space in which to add any supporting information, so use continuation sheets to highlight aspects of your experience and skills which are relevant for the charity's needs
- photocopy the final version
- return the form by the closing date. Organisations with Equal Opportunities policies cannot accept applications after the closing date
- attach your CV if you feel it will add to the information given.

❝ *For my current job (advertised in the Guardian) I filled in a standard application form and had one panel interview with a written test. All candidates were asked the same questions and were scored on their replies.* **❞**

Elice McGreevey, Head of Finance and Administration, Crisis

PRESENTING YOURSELF AT A INTERVIEW

There are two sorts of interviews:
- individual interviews
- panel interviews

The same general guidelines apply to both sorts of interview.

Individual Interviews

These are on a one-to-one basis and can range from a very formal structured interview to a informal chat. You may well have interviews with several people in the same organisation in sequence. Many larger organisations start with a personnel interview and then go on to introduce you to the people you would actually be working with.

Panel Interviews

These are interviews where more than one person interviews you. Panels may contain three, four or five members. In many ways they are more difficult than individual interviews. There may well be a dynamic going on between members of the panel which probably has nothing to do with you. Be sensitive to this and realise that this is a game you cannot enter into.

Bear in mind the following the points:

- try not to exclude anybody on the panel
- respond initially to the person who ask you the question instead of looking around the room at everybody
- if you find one person is consistently asking all the questions, you may want to try to draw the other panel members in. They may feel they can't get a word in otherwise.

> **"** *I saw the job advertised in my local paper – the Ham and High – as well as the Jewish Chronicle. I had to fill in a very extensive application form which asked things like 'why do you think you should apply for this post?' I had to attend two interviews. The first was a group of ten – we had to break into pairs and then debate as a complete group. We were observed by five people. For the second interview, there was a panel of three people – my future line manager and two members of the Management Committee. The first question, which I really did anticipate, was how would I manage with the children when they were ill and on holiday. I tried to think out my answers before speaking and to keep them reasonably succinct.* **"**
> Trisha Ward, co-ordinator, Holocaust Survivors Centre

GUIDELINES FOR A SUCCESSFUL INTERVIEW

Preliminary Planning

- make sure you know your CV backwards – this will be all they know about you and their questions will probably be based on it
- find out all you can about the organisation. Ask to be sent a copy of the Annual Report or any relevant publication
- ring up and ask who will be interviewing you. If it's a panel interview, ask for their positions in the organisation – it will give you a clue to the type and level of questions
- anticipate some of the possible questions and practice your answers with your 'buddy'
- obtain the agreement of people who are willing to act as referees for you. See that they are appropriate people for the particular job application.

Creating a Good First Impression

- decide what points you want to put across at the interview and what impression you want to make
- be on time – ring up for directions in advance if you're not sure
- dress presentably. You're not expected to wear designer suits in the voluntary sector but you should look clean and tidy. Wear clothes that are appropriate and comfortable.
- most people are nervous at interviews but a smile and a confident handshake can go a along way to overcoming this.

In the Interview

- find a relaxed but alert position to sit in and try not to move too much
- avoid yes/no answers but don't overwhelm the interviewer with too much detail. Keep answers short and to the point
- don't be afraid to ask for clarification if you don't understand a question. If you find a question is too general, e.g. "tell me about your career to date" – ask them to be more specific
- turn negatives into positives e.g., "Yes I failed Biology but that's when I realised I had a flair for computers"
- make sure you get across the things that make you stand out, e.g. voluntary experience, special skills, qualifications etc. You've every right to be proud of them

THE FIVE 'P'S

Remember: PRIOR PREPARATION PROMOTES POSITIVE PERFORMANCE

Prior – take time to research your options, your possibilities and the voluntary sector

Preparation – spend time preparing your application. Make it stand out from the crowd

Promotes – promote yourself on your CV – it's your personal ambassador – and in accompanying letters

Positive – remember that every negative situation can be changed around to present its positive side. Be positive!

Performance – rehearse and practice your interview techniques until you are really confident.

- make eye contact as much as possible with your interviewer. If it's a panel interview, you may want to respond initially to your questioner and then make eye contact with the other members of the panel.

At the end of the Interview

- prepare some questions for the end, e.g. what training is available? what are the promotion prospects?
- ask about salary at the end if this has not already been dealt with earlier
- when can I expect to hear? is a reasonable question
- if you don't get the job, you any want to write or telephone asking if they will explain why you were unsuccessful. You may be able to glean useful pointers from them.

" I was officially appointed after I had been doing the job six months. The job was advertised, I sent in my CV and went through a formal interview process. This was because of Equal Opportunities. At the interview I was as psyched-up as I have ever been at any job interview. I found it harder because I had been working alongside the people interviewing me. "

Sheenagh Day, Fundraising Manager, Family Planning Association

Equal Opportunities

Most of the guidelines given above assume that you do not know the people who are going to be interviewing you.

Sometimes funding is made available for a permanent post for a job already in existence. You may have been doing the job as a volunteer or in a paid temporary capacity. Equal Opportunities means that jobs which are re-structured have to be advertised in order to give everyone a fair chance.

If you apply for the newly established post you will then have to go through a formal selection procedure. This often involves being interviewed by people you have been working with. Although it can be difficult to be interviewed by colleagues:

- try to maintain a balance between being formal and being relaxed

- prepare for the interview in the same way you would if you didn't know the people
- remember that, if you have done the job satisfactorily for a while, the chances are high that you will be appointed

And finally, good luck!

USEFUL PUBLICATIONS

The Voluntary Agencies Directory, Bedford Square Press

Directory of Volunteering and Employment Opportunities, by Jan Brownfoot and Frances Wilks, Directory of Social Change.

Both these publications contain useful background information and should be available in most public libraries or from the **Directory of Social Change**.

5
GETTING A FIRST JOB: OPPORTUNITIES FOR YOUNG PEOPLE

Are you about to leave school? Or about to graduate? Have you found work yet? Do you know what you want to do? If you are still deciding what sort of career or job is right for you, or are still seeking that elusive first job, why not consider employment, whether paid or unpaid, in a voluntary organisation?

Britain's voluntary sector now employs between an estimated 438,000 and 482,000 paid staff (full-and part-time) or over 2% of total employment, and contributes nearly 4% to the gross domestic product (GDP). It is more important to the economy than either motor manufacturing or farming. Each year around 23 million people volunteer in charities and other not-for-profit organisations, contributing more than five billion hours of their time. The voluntary sector offers challenging and rewarding career opportunities, together with appropriate career structures. Many of the professional and vocational skills required by the sector are similar to those needed by private and public sector organisations. Some, such as fund raising, are more specialised.

FINDING A FIRST JOB IN THE VOLUNTARY SECTOR

If you:

- have **commitment** and **enthusiasm**,
- are willing to **work hard** for pay which may not be as generous as in other sectors,

- have **skills** you can offer, and
- are prepared to take **further training** if necessary,

then you may find a voluntary organisation offers just the right kind of first job for you. Although it is easier to get a job if you have previous work experience, many charities count volunteer work as relevant experience. If you are having trouble getting your first job, volunteering for a charity could give you valuable experience, prove your commitment, and find you in the right place at the right time if a paid job becomes available, as well as keeping you occupied in a job, doing something useful, and sustaining or even enhancing your skills.

How to find the Right Organisation?

You will need to think flexibly and be prepared to do something possibly quite different from the subjects you did perhaps for your degree or vocational training. You will also need to decide which is the right kind of voluntary organisation for you. As there are about 500,000 not-for-profit organisations in Britain, covering between them almost every conceivable subject you can think of, the choice is wide. How can you find which organisation is most appropriate for you? The answer lies in considering what your interests are:

- Do you like animals, or people?
- Are you a sports lover?
- Are you concerned about the environment or about helping people in need?
- Do you want to find out more about other parts of the world?
- Do you want to develop linguistic skills?
- Do you enjoy word processing and technology, or prefer working with people?
- Do you like talking to people on the telephone, perhaps as a counsellor, or do you prefer working face to face?

Once you have decided which of your interests you would most like to pursue, you will then need to undertake some research to help you decide which organisations to consider and to find out what opportunities exist. See *Chapters 2 and 4* for information and suggestions on how to do this. There are also various directories available which list voluntary organisations, outlining their aims and objectives and the work they do (see the end of this chapter for some of these). You could also ask your school or college careers advisory service – some are now working with voluntary organisations to identify work opportunities for graduates and young people.

How else to find out about types of Work Possibilities?

As part of your research into the sorts of jobs available and the kinds of experience and qualifications needed in the voluntary sector, you will need to look in the general and specialist press and other media. See *Chapter 4* for details.

If you are seeking a first job you would face very tough competition if you apply for positions advertised in newspapers, as these will almost certainly be aimed at people with experience. Rejections to your applications may prove very disheartening. However, if you have some relevant voluntary experience, you may be lucky enough to be called for an interview. This can only be beneficial for you, both as part of a learning process and to give you confidence in dealing with interview situations. You might even be offered the job! If not, the organisation may keep details about you on record in case another vacancy arises.

The Importance of Volunteering

Because the 'culture' of the Voluntary Sector is different from that of the public and private sectors, many charities will only consider people who have had some sort of experience in voluntary organisations, whether paid or unpaid. If you have no previous employment experience, it is essential when applying for a job that you highlight any voluntary work you have been involved in and the skills you have gained from it. This is particularly important when you are a recent graduate, looking for your first job or wanting to switch very early in your working life from a career in the private or public sector to one in the voluntary sector. It doesn't matter whether your voluntary work was rattling a tin for a charity, taking part in a sponsored swim at school, going on a conservation holiday during school or college vacations, being a Girl Guide or Boy Scout, helping out in a local home for disabled people or chairing your college Rag Committee – it all counts. So make sure you emphasise what you did and what you learnt from it.

> In your CV, highlight any voluntary work you have done, and the skills you have gained.

> **"** My advice to graduates looking for a first job is to try volunteering. I couldn't bear the thought of graduating and not doing anything. If you volunteer, you're not sitting around at home but honing up your skills and learning new skills. And volunteering is so worthwhile. **"**
>
> Sarah Staunton, Volunteer Officer, BTCV

If you do not have previous employment experience, other features of your life become much more important in getting work – such as showing commitment, an aptitude for leadership, innovative ideas, or success in fundraising, communication or using your initiative. This is why volunteering can be a bridge into employment. You will have the opportunity to develop your skills. You will be able to show that there are organisations whose causes and aims you support. And you might even be in the know when vacancies occur.

> **"** After I graduated with a degree in chemistry and a post-graduate qualification in computing, I couldn't find work. So I did voluntary work for Victim Support, and then later I joined ChildLine as a volunteer counsellor. I've done various counselling courses and seem to have a knack for counselling. I've decided to continue with my voluntary counselling work, and out of it has come a part-time paid job working in an alcohol advisory service. **"**
>
> 'Sid', Volunteer Counsellor with ChildLine

Volunteering also gives you an edge beyond having qualifications and a basic CV (Curriculum Vitae). If getting the particular job you want, or getting any employment at all, is proving difficult, it is always better to be doing something than nothing, providing what you do is relevant to what you want to do. You can also be earning a bit more money than just getting basic income support. Many organisations using unemployed volunteers put them onto the Government's Employment Training (ET) schemes so that all transport and out-of-pocket expenses are covered and there can be a top-up to benefit income.

If you are under 18 and not in full-time education or a job you can get a place on a Youth Training scheme, or on other training courses, and be working towards a National Vocational Qualification (NVQ). 16 and 17 year olds have the right to training that pays them while they learn and work. Various schemes and courses covering a wide range of future careers are available, many of them run in conjunction with **Training and Enterprise Councils** (TECs) which approve the training providers. Work placements, an integral part of the training, are found locally and include voluntary organisations which become involved in the training. Qualifications are accredited and awarded by such recognised bodies as **City and Guilds**, the **Royal Society of Arts** (RSA) and the **British Technical Education Council** (BTEC).

TECs also fund **Employment Action** projects that enable unemployed people to stay in the world of work, maintain job skills through relevant work experience, gain a current job reference and contribute to the community. Your abilities are matched to the needs of a local organisation which can include voluntary groups. You undertake temporary voluntary work and learn new skills such as computing or youth and community work too. Employment Action, an equal opportunities programme, pays you the equivalent of your current benefit entitlement, plus £10 a week and helps with

> " I did a History degree at university. I went on some British Trust for Conservation Volunteers, BTCV, Natural Break holidays during vacations and did a leadership training course. I'd volunteered in the past and been a Girl Guide at school. I decided I wanted to work in conservation, but I didn't have the right degree and after I graduated there were thousands of others like me looking for jobs. So I joined BTCV as a voluntary field officer under the Employment Training Scheme. Now I'm at head office as a volunteer officer for publicity and fundraising, getting specific experience and training in those areas. BTCV is making sure I make the best use of my time and learn what I want to. I'm part of a team and I have responsibility for setting up a national data base of all BTCV's projects.
>
> I'm on income support and I get my travel expenses. Financially its difficult, but it's such a good opportunity to get experience and training in conservation. You have to be committed and not too bothered about material things. If I didn't believe in what I was doing I wouldn't do it. And there's always the possibility of paid employment. I stand in good stead because I'm on site and getting trained. "
>
> Sarah Staunton, Volunteer Officer, BTCV

travel and any child care costs. You must be aged 18 and above and have been claiming unemployment benefit or income support for six months to be eligible. Placements are usually for six months but can last up to twelve. **Community Action** projects provide part-time placement opportunities in such areas as office skills, building and maintenance, and home services for people who have been unemployed and claiming benefit for more than a year. Voluntary and charitable organisations are usually the main providers of Community Action opportunities.

Ask at your local Training and Enterprise Council (TEC), Careers Office or Jobcentre for details about any of the government schemes which are organised and run by the Employment Service. The Employment Service offers a range of services, including advice, job search seminars and job clubs, as well as training, to people who are seeking work, and it pays benefit while they are looking. It also provides information on setting up your own business, if that is something that appeals. Look in the phone book under '*Employment Service*' for how to contact it in your area. Many locally based organisations, which may themselves be charities, also provide help, advice and training including through contracts with TECs, and run government projects such as Employment Action and Jobplan Workshops, for people who are unemployed. The **Bridge Project** in Tower Hamlets, which serves the whole of East London, is one of these. Ask your local library, council or job centre for details of any in your own area.

If you are unemployed, you volunteer and you are not put on a government scheme, the Inland Revenue and Department of Social Security (DSS) have various regulations concerning when expenses and other payments become 'earnings', including in relation to income support and unemployment benefit. Check with the organisation what it is prepared to pay you and, if in doubt, ask at your local job centre too. You must also inform your local Benefits Agency office that you are volunteering. For further details see the Volunteer Centre UK's publications "*All Expenses Paid*" by Angela Whitcher (1992) and "*Volunteers' Welfare Benefits and Taxation*" (1992), and the Benefit Agency's leaflet "*Voluntary and Part-time Workers*". Remember also to advise the organisation for which you volunteer if you are obliged to be available for work under Unemployment Benefit rules. The rules generally can be complex and difficult to understand so it is worth getting help and guidance.

What else must I do?

Once you have done your research and made some decisions about which voluntary causes and organisations you would like to get involved with, you will need to draw up a CV and develop a job search strategy.

Your CV is your key marketing tool. A well laid out, well presented CV is vital as the first step in progressing from applicant to interviewee. Yet many young people have difficulty in laying out and presenting a CV in an attractive, user-friendly way. Research shows that, on average, it takes a personnel officer just four seconds to decide whether to reject a CV or not. So, you must get your message over quickly and convincingly. See *Appendix 1 and 2* for tips.

Some useful guides have been published on how to write CVs. The University of London Careers Advisory Service has one available for purchase called *How to Write Curriculum Vitae*.

DEVISING A JOB STRATEGY

When looking for your first job in the voluntary sector there are two main strategies you can follow. You can either:

- target particular posts which you see advertised or hear about in specific organisations OR you can

- 'spray and pray' – send out your CV with a covering letter 'on spec' to those organisations in which you would like to work.

Devise a job strategy. You may strike lucky. But persistence also pays.

Or you could do both. Whatever you decide to do, you will need to be prepared for rejection letters. In general, voluntary organisations do not welcome speculative letters and applications, and staff do not have time to give specific advice. But some do welcome and respond to letters out of the blue. And you may strike lucky, having first the skills they need and need urgently. Persistence also pays. However, if you have identified certain organisations you would really like to work for it may be useful to contact their personnel department or representative. You may be able to meet them and find out about the possibilities. You may also be able to join in a voluntary capacity. For more information on job strategies see *Chapter 4*.

Many organisations are now using application forms, either as well as, or instead of, CVs. This is partly because of the requirements of having adopted an equal opportunities policy, as it means that all applicants answer the same questions and provide the same information about themselves. The application forms can then be more easily compared than individual CVs. See *Chapter 4* for further details.

Again there are some useful publications available to purchase, including **London University Careers Advisory Service's** "*How to Complete an Application Form*".

If you are among those called for interview, remember the five 'P's:

PRIOR

PREPARATION

PROMOTES

POSITIVE

PERFORMANCE

Research and prepare for your interview. Find out everything you can about the organisation through its own literature (Annual Report, leaflets, etc.), through any press items, by asking around. Think what sort of questions you might be asked, prepare your answers, and consider what you want to ask the organisation about – career prospects, training opportunities, benefits, and so on.

If you need further guidance on how to go about finding a job, the University of London Careers Advisory Service offers a comprehensive careers guidance and information service for all graduates, not only those from the University of London's own colleges. The service includes aptitude tests and interviews with careers advisers and the charges are reasonable. Check with your own college to see if it offers something similar.

One other alternative exists to trying to find a job in an already established organisation – you could set up your own business and become self employed! With the burgeoning 'contract culture' between statutory authorities and voluntary agencies, numerous opportunities are developing for people to provide services to the voluntary sector on a project or short-term contract basis. Various business start-up schemes are available – TECs can assist you with these. See too *Chapter 13* for further details. You could also contact organisations such as the **Prince's Youth Business Trust**, part of the **Prince's Trust**, which helps young people, including those with disabilities, to set up in business by offering finance through loans and grants, and advice.

POSSIBILITIES FOR VOLUNTARY WORK

The importance of undertaking voluntary work to help you in seeking your first job, or as your first job even though it is unpaid, cannot be over-stressed. There are various opportunities as many voluntary organisations, covering a wide range of activities and interests, are keen to recruit volunteers. See *Chapter 3* for details on volunteering. Some organisations offer long-term positions so you can fill a 'gap' year and gain valuable experience, while also supplementing your benefits. The Government's Employment Training, Employment Action and Community Action schemes have already been mentioned. If you want to volunteer overseas there are also various possibilities, both on short-term and long-term projects – *see Chapter 10*.

A VOLUNTEER'S STORY – BARNEY STRINGER

"I graduated with a BSc in Physics and Philosophy. I had no idea what I wanted to do when I left university. I had already had a year off before doing my degree. So I did some temporary jobs and went travelling in Africa. But I felt I must find something and get some career direction. I was interested in transport so I wrote to the London Cycling Campaign and Transport 2000, and also went on doing British Trust for Conservation Volunteers (BTCV) projects, which I'd done in university holidays. Then Transport 2000 asked me in for a chat. I said I could help them with desk top publishing and that I'd like to work on their magazine. I started as a volunteer one day a week, then built up to three. At first I stuffed envelopes. Then they let me use the computers, help produce the magazine and do some writing. Now I've moved on to sub-editing, design and layout too. I was also able to go on the Employment Training (ET) Scheme, so Transport 2000 was able to invest in me more and give me more responsibility and challenges.

Since the ET Scheme finished I've stayed on as a volunteer while looking for paid work. I enjoy it very much, it's useful to say I'm doing it and it keeps me sane. I'm actively seeking employment now, applying for jobs I see advertised to do with transport, and I've been called for interviews. I've gained so much experience from working at Transport 2000. It's helped me a great deal.

My advice to others would be that it's very worthwhile to volunteer as I did, especially as an alternative to being unemployed. But it shouldn't be a substitute for looking for paid work."

Another possibility if you are a recent graduate, perhaps with little experience but some idea of what you may want to do, is to undertake further training which includes a placement, perhaps in a charity. Various courses are available, including those run by organisations such as **Working for a Charity** and **C.I.T.E. (Associates) Ltd** – Commercial & Industrial Training for Employment. Working for a Charity offers a course of seminars, together with a charity placement, to help you understand how the voluntary sector works. Although you will have to pay, the fees are not large and you may be able to obtain funding or perhaps get a relative to pay.

CITE's courses include personal and professional development programmes like the ET Graduate Gateway scheme, designed to enable recent graduates to gain an overview of an organisation's different functions, develop personal qualities, and break into the job market. Trainees undertake work experience, which can be in a charity, within their chosen career area. A similar scheme is run by **Charity Action**, where unemployed trainees are called 'Actioneers' and are placed with a charity for periods of three months up to one year. If you are on a voluntary placement of whatever

> **“** After teaching English abroad I decided to return to Britain and make a career change. I applied for a wide range of jobs but couldn't get an interview. I needed to decide what I wanted to do and get relevant experience, but normal voluntary work would have affected my benefit. So I joined the ET Graduate Gateway scheme at CITE (Associates) Ltd after seeing an advertisement in **The Guardian**. It would allow me to work and continue to receive benefit plus a training allowance of £10 a week and some travel costs.
>
> As I continued to do research for jobs, my interest in the voluntary sector grew. I sent off for job descriptions of posts advertised in **The Guardian**, including one at the Directory of Social Change (DSC). I needed to find a placement as part of the training scheme, so I contacted the DSC. They offered me a placement as assistant to the Courses and Conferences Manager. I received an excellent induction, on-the-job training and limitless support. After two months I was offered a permanent position.**”**
>
> Kathleen Gillett, Directory of Social Change

type, you might also consider getting extra qualifications through distance learning courses. The RSA runs two courses relevant to working in voluntary organisations: 'Management in the Voluntary Sector' and 'Counselling Skills'. Other options are offered by the **National Extension College** (NEC). If eventually, you decide you want to stay in the voluntary sector and take advanced qualifications, the **Open University** has a Voluntary Sector Management Programme that includes certificate and diploma courses such as 'Managing Voluntary and Non-profit Enterprises' and 'Winning resources and Support', the 'first accredited course on fundraising, public relations and campaigning to be presented by a British university'.

Community Service Volunteers (CSV)

CSV, the national volunteer agency, welcomes volunteers of all ages, backgrounds and skills, to play an active part in their community, working face to face with people in need. It organises a variety of programmes to involve those who want to volunteer, including graduates, school leavers and young offenders. CSV believes everyone has something to offer the community and challenges young people to experience the rewards, hard work and fun of working as volunteers.

Everyone is welcome, no one is rejected. CSV actively seeks the energy, enthusiasm and commitment of younger volunteers. This includes those who are unemployed, and/or homeless. CSV's innovative national youth training initiative 'Service Away from Home' for young people aged 16-18 provides 'at risk' young people with training (leading to City and Guilds vocational qualifications in community care), accommodation, support and security. Trainees acquire new skills and live independently while helping others in the community.

CSV's full-time volunteer programme for younger people aged 16 to 35 guarantees a placement for everyone who wants one. Each placement:

- is full-time and away from home
- is four months minimum to 12 months maximum
- provides full board, accommodation and travel costs
- pays weekly travel money/allowance
- has supervision on the project and backup from CSV

> **Until July 1992 I was a full-time student studying Social Psychology and Social Administration. I wanted to apply the subjects to work. Volunteering seemed the best way of gaining invaluable practical experience and working with different client groups. My placement as a Community Service Volunteer in a residential home for mentally and physically frail older people, has more than met my expectations. The work has given me the chance to become part of a team, but also the opportunity to use my own initiative.**
>
> **I have met some wonderful people and learned a lot about the needs of older people with dementia. As a volunteer I have gained the same experience as I would have done in paid employment. But perhaps most importantly, volunteering has given me the confidence to know that I can do the job well! It has helped me to develop personally and professionally. I am now in the fortunate position of preparing for several interviews – interviews which six months ago I probably would not have been invited to.**
>
> Janet Bell, former CSV volunteer

> **I am a Community Service Volunteer on a Young Disabled Unit at a hospital. It provides regular or occasional periods of care, and also accepts newly disabled people. I became a volunteer simply because I wanted to do something other than college for a while.**
>
> **Becoming a CSV was a real eye opener. 'Life experience' that's the most accurate way to describe it. I certainly feel stronger and more confident now. I wouldn't have missed this experience for anything. I feel it was more worthwhile than a year at college or at work. What you receive in return is more than you give.**
>
> Marie Kerrigan, CSV volunteer

> You can apply at any time and the more flexible you are about where you are placed in the country, and on what sort of project, the quicker a placement will be found.

British Trust for Conservation Volunteers

BTCV (British Trust for Conservation Volunteers) is another organisation which welcomes volunteers. It provides them with the opportunity to learn new skills and receive full training and support, while helping to protect and improve their environment.

Through its annual programme of international conservation working holidays BTCV offers volunteers the chance to learn about and participate in conservation projects overseas whether creating footpaths in a seashore national park in Cape Cod or a tree planting safari in the mountainous deserts of Andalucia. BTCV also has links with similar organisations overseas, such as the **Australian Trust for Conservation Volunteers** (ATCV). It is sometimes possible to get placements overseas in organisations like ATCV, particularly through voluntary agencies like **GAP Activity Projects**.

> ### A Volunteer's Story – Lou Wardle
> Lou began a business studies degree with an ambition to become an accountant. While at college she began volunteering with BTCV by taking part in Natural Break conservation working holidays. She enjoyed it so much she gave up her course and became a full-time volunteer leader of environmental projects.
>
> She spent four years volunteering and learnt a full range of conservation skills. She is now working in a paid BTCV post, creating a wildlife and conservation area on the site of a former sewage works in Ystragyndlys, Wales. She involves volunteers from around the area in her projects.

BTCV's network of over 90 offices throughout England, Wales and Northern Ireland offers young people (and others) numerous short-term volunteer opportunities such as Natural Break conservation working holidays. You could make a longer term commitment by working as a Volunteer Officer for BTCV, thereby taking up a unique opportunity to develop your practical, communication and management skills, an ideal chance to progress your career within the environmental field.

Most BTCV Volunteer Officers work, like Lou Wardle, at a local BTCV office to learn about practical conservation. Many subsequently also obtain jobs as BTCV field officers, working around Britain. Occasionally an opportunity may arise to apply for a post at head office.

> I studied English Literature at university and then taught English in France. While there I saw an advertisement for a job as a creative writer in conservation in Yorkshire and decided conservation was what I really wanted to do. So I returned to Yorkshire. I was told the only way in without a relevant degree was volunteering. I found BTCV and the Yorkshire Wildlife Trust in the phone book and started volunteering for both. Soon afterwards a position became available with the BTCV project in York for a full-time trainee. With their help I managed to get on Employment Training which pays you a basic income plus all travel expenses. I was immediately given responsibility for local publicity and fundraising and did practical conservation work. I also went on courses paid for by BTCV. In six months I met many other people who worked for North Yorkshire's countryside projects, as well as private landowners, and was treated as an equal even though I was volunteering. Then the job as Appeals Administrator came up at BTCV head office.
>
> I applied, had a competitive interview and got it. It's full-time, paid and there are prospects for promotion. Now I'm training as a fundraiser. BTCV are very keen on training people, and I can get my qualifications with them. I enjoy it and I feel as though I'm making a contribution to conservation and working for a common cause that I'm committed to.
>
> My advice to any graduate or anyone who is unemployed or uncertain what to do is to go and try volunteering and find out what you like. You don't need a CV to volunteer. People only want to know that you are enthusiastic and want to try. Just show commitment and people will give you opportunities.
>
> Jim Boot, Appeals Administrator, BTCV

SOURCES OF HELP AND INFORMATION

Publications/Magazines

All Expenses Paid, by Angela Whitcher (published by the Volunteer Centre UK, 1992)

Charity Choice (published by Abercorn Hill Associates)

Charity Magazine (contact the Charities Aid Foundation)

Directory of Volunteer & Employment Opportunities (published by Directory of Social Change)

Third Sector, the news magazine for people in the charity world (published by Art Publishing International)

University of London Careers Advisory Service – various publications including "*How to Write a Curriculum Vitae*" and "*How to Complete an Application Form*", available from 50 Gordon Square, London WC1H 0PQ, tel: 071-387 8221

Voluntary Agencies Directory (published by Bedford Square Press)

Volunteers' Welfare Benefits and Taxation (published by the Volunteer Centre UK)

Specialist Recruitment Agencies

CR Charity Recruitment, 40 Rosebery Avenue, London EC1R 4RN, tel: 071-833 0770

Charity Appointments, 3 Spitals Yard, London E1 6AQ, tel: 071-247 4502

Charity People, Suite 308, The Chandlery, 50 Westminster Bridge Road, London SE1 7QY, tel: 071-721 7585

Training Courses

C.I.T.E. (Associates) Ltd, 23 Newman Street, London W1P 3HA, Tel: 071-636 5544

Institute of Charity Fundraising Managers, Market Towers, 1 Nine Elms Lane, London SW8 5NQ, tel: 071-627 3436

Working for a Charity, 44-46 Caversham Road, London NW5 2DS, tel: 071-911 0353

Other Useful Information

Bridge Project, 144 Cambridge Heath Road, Bethnal Green, London E1 5QJ, tel: 071-790 5579

British Trust for Conservation Volunteers, Head Office, 36 St Mary's Street, Wallingford, Oxon OX10 0EU, tel: 0491-39766

Charity Action, 3 Down Place, Hammersmith, London W6 9JH

Charityfair – an annual event run by the Directory of Social Change at the Business Design Centre in London in March each year includes a Volunteering and Employment Forum

Community Service Volunteers, CSV, 237 Pentonville Road, London N1 9NJ, tel: 071-278 6601

Industrial Society, Robert Hyde House, 48 Bryanston Square, London W1H 7LN, tel: 071-839 3898

National Extension College, 18 Brooklands Avenue, Cambridge CB2 2HN, tel: 0223-316644

The Open University, Customer Service Centre, PO Box 222, Walton Hall, Milton Keynes MK7 6YY, tel: 0908-653473/ 655182

The Prince's Trust and **The Royal Jubilee Trusts**, 8 Bedford Row, London WC1R 4BA, tel: 071-430 0524

Royal Society of Arts (RSA), Westwood Way, Coventry CV4 8HS, tel: 0203-470033

Training and Enterprise Councils (TECs) – check your local telephone directory

6
EMPLOYEE VOLUNTEERING AND SECONDMENT

These are two different activities both of which involve the encouragement and support of your employer.

Employee volunteer programmes involve employees contributing time to the voluntary sector. This can be done individually or by groups of employees either in company time or in employees' own time or a combination of both.

Secondment is a work commitment and involves an employer paying the salary of a staff member while they work, usually on a specific project, in a voluntary organisation. This can be short term or long term. The usual maximum length is for two years. It can also relate to a particular task or the employees's particular skills.

They are significant ways in which both individuals and businesses can contribute to the community. They are also ways in which the volunteer can take on new roles and gain new skills (e.g. in chairing meetings) outside the workplace, which will enhance a CV (Curriculum Vitae) and the prospects of promotion. For those thinking about or actually seeking a new career in the voluntary sector, employee volunteering or secondment can provide useful experience, the time to consider what might be an appropriate next step and added value to a CV.

Some employers have set up volunteering and secondment schemes. If this is the case, you should approach the relevant manager with a request to participate. If there is no scheme, this is something that you might like to raise through appropriate channels. You can get background information and advice on this from **Business in the Community** (for Employee volunteering) or **Action Resource Centre** (ARC) for secondment. The addresses of these organisations are given at the end of the chapter. Together they produce a newsletter aimed at employees called 'Working Out'.

EMPLOYEE VOLUNTEERING

Volunteering is essentially a personal commitment, but companies and large organisations can facilitate employee volunteering by:

- support and recognition for voluntary activities
- identifying and matching community needs with employee volunteers
- developing specific company projects
- providing resources for community activities.

Sometimes, the initiative will come from the employer, sometimes from an employee, or group of employees. There is no limit to the different sorts of voluntary activity that can be undertaken. If you take on the responsibility of being on an employee volunteering committee, you may like to bear in mind the following:

- be clear who you are trying to help e.g., local community, disabled groups, young people, ex-offenders etc. You may not always want to stick to these groups but it can be helpful to have a policy
- draw up a skills bank so that you can match individual skills with specific needs
- be realistic about the time people can give
- be sensitive in approaching potential volunteers – no-one should feel coerced
- make sure there are lots of opportunities for fun.

If there isn't already an employee volunteering scheme in your company you might like to suggest that one is started. Other companies have noticed the following benefits:

- raising of employee morale
- bridging of the gap between what the company does for the community and what employees do
- improvement in community relations

" We set up employee volunteering in Liverpool about two years ago. At first it was difficult. People said that they worked hard enough for their pay and that the company couldn't take up their free time, that sort of thing. That changed when people saw us doing things in the local community. They saw it wasn't a publicity stunt and that it was a success – then they wanted to be involved as well.

Our first contact was with a local school. We approached the first year and asked them to run a competition to design a logo for us. They did and also invented a name for us, which we've used ever since – REACH OUT. We presented the boy who designed the logo with a book voucher and we were able to donate a computer to the school my old computer – I was having a new one. A group of us went over to train them on it in the lunch hour.

We do a variety of things. Today a local policeman asked us to support the canine division's sponsored walk and we bought a page of advertising in their brochure. We've been involved with setting up a Charity Golf Day for a local children's hospice. One of our members even flew a plane for a local charity. We help our local community but we don't focus exclusively on it.

We don't just give money. We're also keen to give hands-on practical help. I chair a committee with nine members. A Body Bank has been set up which is a group of people who are willing to take on almost any physical task.

It's done a lot for all of us. I've met a lot of other people in Whitbreads I probably wouldn't ever have met otherwise. I also realise that there are many people in the world much less fortunate than myself. I get a buzz out of doing something to help and I enjoy making new relationships. It does mean that I have less time, particularly at the weekends. I've involved the whole family. My five year old is going to be doing a treasure hunt for charity soon.

The idea goes from strength to strength – it's brought people together, not just in the community but from management down to shop floor in Whitbreads."

Barbara Freeman, Site Services Assistant, Whitbread PLC

- more opportunities for staff to practice and develop business skills – especially leadership, teamwork, decision making and customer relations
- better communication and understanding between the people in different departments in an organisation.

Business Volunteering

Some employee volunteering schemes involve using the employees specific business skills. This is sometimes called business volunteering. Schemes include **Lawyers in the Community** and **Chartered Accountants in the Community**.

Sometimes companies are approached directly by a voluntary organisation because they have the skills that the charity needs. If you take part in this kind of volunteering, you may like to remember:

- that the circumstances in which you do your voluntary work may be very different from the circumstances in which you do your job
- that in certain circumstances you may not have the time or the budget to do what you would do for a commercial client
- to negotiate with the voluntary organisation and define clearly what they want you to do and what budget and back-up, if any, is available.

Despite the difficulties, there can be many rewards, including:

- personal development and a sense of achievement
- greater understanding and increased tolerance of others
- broadening of existing skills and increased confidence
- an opportunity to work in a team
- realisation of how well resourced and organised the business sector can be.

Touche Ross were approached to provide training for prisoners in Pentonville Prison. The company developed a 'Back-to-work' training programme, including interview practice, help with filling in application forms and confidence building courses. These were designed to be part of a pre-release package.

All the volunteers are staff support trainers and Touche Ross give six days of their time each year. Each volunteer had a different idea of what the prison would actually be like when they went there for the first time.

The training had to take place in a small, rather hot room with frequent interruptions. Many of the prisoners found it hard to concentrate because of the environment. Despite this, the volunteer trainers found it a very rewarding and educative experience.

Heather Dallas, the co-ordinator said, "we recognise that there is a terrific need for people to build up their confidence in dealing with the outside world after years in prison. Their self-esteem is very low and they need to get used to making decisions again. One person said it had helped just to hear someone call him by his first name."

Amongst some the benefits the trainers reported were: ' a sense of achievement in helping people', 'greater understanding of others, 'broadening of our own training skills' and 'a sense of gratitude at realising how well resourced and organised we are.'

SECONDMENT

Secondment is the loan from a business to a charity of an employee on a part- or a full-time basis. Secondees lend their professional skills and business experience to a voluntary organisation. Most frequently they are in the areas of: finance, fundraising, marketing, training, human resources and PR.

There are two sorts of secondment: developmental and transitional. They reflect the different needs of the individual secondee.

If you want to do a secondment, it is worth thinking about:

- what skills you have to offer
- what sort of organisation you would like to work with
- why you want to do it
- the cost to your employer of releasing you to do it
- the personal commitment involved.

Developmental Secondment

These secondments tend to be of a fixed period and are often project based assignments. There are usually undertaken as part of an individual's career development plan. A larger organisation may decide that a manager needs to have a different kind of experience than can be offered in the

> *After 20 years employment with Marks and Spencer and having gained experience in both the Personnel and Commercial areas of the business, I was offered, as a mid career development, the chance of a twelve month secondment with Shelter Trading Ltd.*
>
> *Shelter Trading Ltd. is the commercial arm of Shelter, the National Campaign for Homeless People. The aim of my secondment was to give me the opportunity of developing my skills and to provide Shelter Trading the benefits of my retail experience.*
>
> *I am now halfway through my year's secondment as the Commercial Trading Manager for Shelter Trading. As I had only ever worked for Marks and Spencer's, it has been particularly useful for me to gain experience of a different culture. The difference is not was great as I had expected but I have developed many new skills, including the basics of accountancy, learning how to type my own letters, and finding out how to set up my own business systems. I am much more self-sufficient.*
>
> *Anyone who is considering secondment must be able to identify fully with the aims of the organisation they are joining. They must also be prepared to become fully involved with the organisation. For me this has meant rattling a collecting tin, volunteering on a telephone helpline after a television programme and attending a reception for donors at venues such as the House of Lords.*
>
> *Working at Shelter has changed many of my perceptions on homelessness. I am now aware of the scale of the problem – there are around two million people homeless in Britain today and that the majority of young homeless people are in that situation through no fault of their own, over 40% have come out of care.*
>
> *I would definitely recommend secondment to anyone. It is important to know that when I return to Marks and Spencer there is a job for me. However, having faced the challenges of the last twelve months and with the new skills that I have developed I will be able to make a much bigger contribution and be more able to cope with future challenges.*

Jane Parry, secondee from Marks & Spencer to Shelter Trading.

company. For example, a manager in a large multi-national might need specific experience running a shop. Although the voluntary organisation will benefit, the business will also benefit by having a more developed employee.

Transitional Secondment

This is when an employee goes on secondment as part of a major change in his or her working life – usually redundancy or retirement.

If it is before redundancy it can give an individual exposure to another environment. It can be a very useful way of making a transition to another career, which may be in the voluntary sector.

> *After I was made redundant from my job as a personal manager in a chartered accountants practice I still had five months paid notice. It was suggested that I go on a secondment to a charity. I've been at the Mental Health Foundation, assessing the personnel situation in the organisation. I've come up with some very interesting findings which I shall be putting in a report.*
>
> *You need to be flexible, to be adaptable to a different culture. Be sensitive to things like clothes. Don't expect secretarial support. Don't come with airs and graces and don't talk about how things were organised in your last company. Be humble – ask if you don't know something. Try and go for a briefing first – ask*
>
> - *for a description of your project or job*
> - *about expenses – are they available and how do you claim them?*
> - *about time – what hours will be expected of you?*
>
> *At the initial interview I asked for what I wanted to come out of the secondment which was:*
>
> - *to gain an understanding of mental health in the community*
> - *hands-on experience of with mental health groups*
> - *contact with academic workers in the field.*
>
> *So far, I am achieving all those objectives and the experience is developing my confidence in the skills I've got.*
>
> Ann-Marie Hersh, secondee to the Mental Health Foundation

USEFUL ADDRESSES

Action Resource Centre (ARC) 102 Park Village East, London NW1 3SP, tel: 071-383 2200. (ARC encourages businesses rather than individuals to approach them)

Business in the Community, 8 Stratton Street, London W1X 5FD, tel: 071-629 1600

The Volunteer Centre UK, 29 Lower King's Road, Berkhamsted, Herts HP4 2AB, tel: 0442-873311

Volunteering Development Scotland, 80 Murray Place, Stirling FK8 2BX, tel. 0786-479593.

Note that at the time of writing, Employees in the Community, the employee volunteering unit of Business in the Community, were planning a merger with the Action Resource Centre. The merged body will be in place by mid-1994.

USEFUL PUBLICATIONS

Employees in the Community: Handbook for Action (available from Business in the Community and the Volunteer Centre UK)

Volunteering for Success (available from Business in the Community)

Making the Most of Employee Community Involvement (available from the Volunteer Centre UK).

Working Out (a newsletter published jointly by the Action Resource Centre and Business in the Community).

Understanding Employee Volunteering (available from Business in the Community and the Volunteer Centre, UK).

7
RETURNING TO WORK: OPPORTUNITIES & OPTIONS IN THE VOLUNTARY SECTOR

By the year 2000, 45% of the labour force will be female. Although unemployment may well remain at high levels, there is also a skills shortage. If organisations, including those in the voluntary sector, are to remain competitive, they will have to capitalise on the skills and talents of *all* sections of the workforce. This means that the skills and talents, updated and upgraded where necessary, of women wanting to take the plunge back into employment may be of value to employers.

> **"** I feel women returners face problems of ageism as an employment gap means one is competing with younger people who may be able to offer comparable work experience. There is a need to emphasise the advantages of greater maturity and non-work skills acquired during the intervening years. The main factor is self-belief and maintaining morale. It is essential not to appear demoralised. **"**
>
> Carol Ihnatowicz, Head of Personnel, Family Welfare Association

If you are considering returning to work you will need to rethink a number of matters. Even after a short break from a full-time paid job, it can be difficult to re-adjust to the demands of work. The most important things for you to do are to:

- undertake career life planning and think about the sorts of jobs you would like
- join new networks
- assess what training you need
- consider personal skills training

- examine self-employment as an option
- look at your child care needs and the options available to you
- look at the different options for flexible working hours and work patterns.

Career Life Planning

Before returning to work, it is important to think about what job you want to do. You need to find a job that you are right for and a job that is right for you.

Questions to ask yourself:

- What am I good at? What skills do I have?
- Where am I now? What changes do I want to make?
- What have I achieved during my period out of work (e.g. in the community, through the school, home tasks, part-time work, etc.)?
- What skills do I most enjoy using and where do I want to use them?
- What am I worth, and what sort of salary level should I be looking at?
- If what I want doesn't work out, what alternatives are there?
- How can I find out more information about planning my career?

Networking

A network is a group of individuals who discuss issues and problems, share information and provide each other with support. Setting up a network can be as easy as a group of women getting together regularly to share information on an informal basis.

You can also practice personal networking by building up your contacts and joining new organisations. For more information on networking, see *Chapter 4*.

The Training Scene

Whilst considering returning to work, you may also be thinking about further education or training to give you the qualifications you may have missed out on, perhaps by leaving school early or not taking appropriate examinations.

> **❝** I learnt from other women about the importance of networking. At one training session we were told 'At every opportunity you must tell people what you are trying to achieve and in this way you will achieve it.' I wrote out a brief history of all the contacts in my life – at school, when I worked, etc. – and made a list of who I was still in contact with. Then I wrote a standard letter with a varying introduction asking 'Can you help me and have you any suggestions?' It was amazingly productive. I made lots of contacts in the voluntary sector which helped me to shape what I wanted to do. Now I have the kind of job I want. It's networking that did it. **❞**
>
> Pam Smith, London First

There are many possible options and you might try some of the following organisations which should be available in your local area. Their telephone numbers will be listed in your local telephone directory:

- **Careers Office**
- **Citizens Advice Bureau** (CAB)
- **College of Further Education**
- **Job Centre**
- **Public Library**
- **Training and Enterprise Council** (TEC)

Personal Skills Training

Women who have been out of the work force often find they have neglected their own needs and so must enhance their personal skills.

This may include upgrading personal effectiveness, developing assertiveness, and improving management of time.

The Industrial Society's **Pepperell Department** runs courses in a range of personal skills including:

- assertiveness
- stress management
- time management

- career development
- presentation skills.

Other courses may be offered by Further Education Colleges, Universities and self help groups.

RETURNING TO WORK – DOROTHY'S STORY

"I did the University of Westminster course 'Professional Updating for Women', which was really good. I learnt various skills from it which came in useful! – negotiation, some employment and contract law, assertion and organisation. I re-thought my CV [curriculum vitae] to good effect. We videoed ourselves under interview conditions and then made suggestions for improvement as we saw the playback. The computer familiarisation sub-course was excellent, introducing us to WordPerfect, spreadsheets and Apple Macs.

The best thing was meeting other women. It clearly helped to remove the isolation that women endure after having established a career, but then giving it up for their children. This also re-establishes confidence since women tend to compliment and support each other. Getting up a head of steam for applications and interviews and networking becomes suddenly possible. I would definitely recommend that women returning to their careers go on such courses to re-think and re-structure their careers, to remove rust from skills and, most importantly, to network."

> **"** I did a Women Returners Course at Reading University – one day a week for eight weeks. It included assertiveness training and time management. It also emphasised that it was possible for someone with my skills and background to find paid employment after 15 years out of the work force. After this I joined 'Women in Management' and attended various training sessions including writing CVs, networking and mentoring, confidence building and techniques for interviews. It all added up to motivating me and showing me how to do it through practical techniques. I also went on an intensive course and learnt to word process. I couldn't have got a job without this. **"**
>
> Pam Smith, London First

> " Try to do courses that will hold your interest and that you can manage comfortably, that may be relevant for your future. I completed a three month course at the University of Hertfordshire (formerly Hatfield Polytechnic) called 'New Opportunities for Women'. It helped to identify opportunities that exist for re-entry to education to improve my qualifications, for part-time or full-time employment, for second careers and in the voluntary sector. I also did a basic word-processing course and a foundation year in counselling (one day a week), which have proved invaluable. Then at my job interview, even though the interview panel had never heard of the Working for a Charity course I had done, they were impressed by it."
>
> Trisha Ward, Co-ordinator, Holocaust Survivors Centre

SELF EMPLOYMENT

You may be thinking of starting your own business (and the same skills will be needed if you want to start your own voluntary organisation). It is not as easy as it seems but, if it does work, be prepared for long hours and lots of commitment.

You will need to ask yourself whether you have:

- the right personal and professional skills?
- the appropriate technical, business and interpersonal skills? If you are weak in any areas, get help before you start. You will need assistance to plan every aspect of your business start-up and get it all down on paper. You can get free and confidential advice from your local Enterprise Agency. To find the one nearest to you, phone **Business in the Community** on 071-229 1600.

CHILD CARE

One of the biggest problems facing women returners is that of finding appropriate and affordable childcare. What are possible childcare options?

- **Childminders**: these are individuals who look after your child, usually with other children, in their own home. They must be registered with the local social services. For further information, contact the **National Childminding Association** at 8 Masons Hill, Bromley BR2 9EY, tel: 081-464 6164.

- **Day Nurseries**: these are run by the local authority and are usually restricted to those in difficult circumstances.
- **Workplace Nurseries**: these provide daycare for children under five. Employers may set up their own, share with other employers or reserve places at a local authority nursery.
- **Private Nurseries**: these provide daycare for young children and must be registered with local social services. There are regulations governing the number of children per staff member. This means that the costs are very high: between £60 and £150 per week depending on whether they are being subsidised.
- **Nannies**: a nanny may or may not be trained. There are no regulations about qualifications. A nanny may live in your home or work on a day to day basis. Alternatively you can share a nanny with another mother. Again the costs are high.
- **After School and Holiday Schemes**: these are schemes to cope with children between five and twelve years old. They are open after school hours and during holidays. Some schemes are run by Education Authorities on school premises after school. Some are run by independent charitable organisations. Contact your local authority or the **Kids Clubs Network**, 279-281 Whitechapel Road, London E1, tel: 071-247 3009, for details.

FLEXIBLE WORKING HOURS AND JOB SHARING

If you have caring or other responsibilities, a full time job may not be what you want. You may want to explore various working options.

- **Flexitime**: fixed core hours but hours at either end of the day may be taken flexibly.
- **Part-time**: a shorter working week with pro-rata payment.
- **Job-sharing**: a full-time job is shared between two people. Information on jobshare opportunities is available from **New Ways to Work** (see end of chapter).
- **Home-working**: typically this has included child minding and light assembly work. Nowadays a wider range of

opportunities is available, sometimes involving greater use of technology (and consequently better paid). It may be possible to have a full- or part-time job divided between home and the workplace.

WORKING IN VOLUNTARY ORGANISATIONS

Having thought about what sort of work you want, what skills you can offer, and what sort of working hours you can cope with, you may decide you would like to work for a charity/voluntary organisation.

Of the estimated 482,000 people who work in charities, 65% are women. Work in the voluntary sector should not be seen as a 'soft option' by returners apprehensive about the possibilities of getting a job with a business employer or in the public sphere.

Most jobs in the sector are proper jobs – properly paid (although salaries may be lower than in the commercial and public sectors), with appointments made on the basis of skills and personal qualities.

> **"** I find the voluntary sector very sympathetic to the special needs of women and it has a generally caring ethos. I have been given a great deal of flexibility in organising my working hours. Flexibility is a bonus for women with other commitments too. Conversely I'm sure that part-time workers represent good value to their organisations. **"**
>
> Carol Ihnatowicz, Head of Personnel, Family Welfare Association

You should think about why you want to work for a charity, and then why you want to work for a particular type of charity. Time taken considering the following may help you to clarify your options:

- Which causes do you feel you could be **committed** to?
- Which jobs would use your **current skills** and experience?
- Which organisations might offer you the right **opportunities**?

For information about job opportunities in the voluntary sector see *Chapter 1* and the "*Directory of Volunteering and Employment Opportunities*" also published by the Directory of Social Change.

> **"** The advantages of working in a voluntary organisation are that it is stimulating, confronting, challenging. I am meeting and working with the most remarkable people and with some superb professionals. It's real pioneering work. The disadvantages are that it is terribly demanding and at times very exhausting, emotionally draining. I'm having to work far more hours than I was originally meant to. But with support and setting boundaries I am enjoying the work. **"**
>
> Trisha Ward, Co-ordinator, Holocaust Survivors Centre

GETTING THAT JOB

This will require planning and research, time and even persistence. Here are some tips to get you started:

- draw up a CV (curriculum vitae) which emphasises your skills, your experience of voluntary work and your commitment
- find out about potential employers
- allocate time every day to looking for work
- start a job file
- get your references organised

For further details see the Pepperell Department's *Resource Pack for Women Returners.*

> **"** I sent out my CV. I had two – one chronological and one with my experience grouped under different skills – on two sides of A4. I spent a great deal of time and effort on these, and showed them to others to gain feedback on how they could be improved. You also need to rehearse and prepare like mad for difficult interviews so that you are confident about answering questions. You must be certain about what you want and what your values are. You need to be totally honest and have the courage to sell hard the things that you are good at. **"**
>
> Pam Smith, London First

> **"** I had to fill in a very extensive application form which asked things like 'why do you think you should apply for this post'. But I had a two page CV which I took to the interview and which was able to give additional information and, I have been told, impressed the panel. **"**
>
> Trisha Ward, Co-ordinator, Holocaust Survivors Centre

VOLUNTEERING

If you really do want to work for a charity, volunteering may be a way in. If you are a volunteer you are in a prime position to meet people.

Exactly the same criteria should apply as when you are seeking a paid job. You should not do just anything that's available, but look for something that stretches your abilities and aspirations, and something which will provide you with work experience that will stand you in good stead in your search for a paid position.

An organisation called **Working for a Charity** (WFAC) runs three month courses which involve some training and work experience through a 'job placement' on a volunteer basis. This is an option which might be worth considering.

> **"** I joined the Working for a Charity course and got the work placement I wanted at Business in the Community (BITC). I did a project for them, attended meetings with the CEO (Chief Executive Officer), went to lots of events and met all the top people. After the placement finished they offered me a short piece of monitoring work. It was my first paid employment for 15 years, and it gave me lots of contacts. That's how I got to know about the organisation I now work for. **"**
>
> Pam Smith, London First

> **"** The Working for a Charity course is a three month work experience and training programme which offers participants an opportunity to explore a new career in the charity world. My placement was with the Directory of Social Change where I carried out a survey into how charities make management training decisions. **"**
>
> Patricia Beecham, Brent Crossroads

USEFUL ORGANISATIONS

The Pepperell Department, The Industrial Society, 48 Bryanston Square, London W1H 7LN, tel: 071-262 2401

The Industrial Society helps develop individual potential for those at work. It has a membership of 16,000 organisations. The Pepperell Department promotes career development and training for women at work. It has just started the Pepperell Network to expand women's training and career options. It has also produced a resource pack for women returners.

New Ways to Work, 309 Upper Street, London N1 2TY, tel: 071-226 4026

New Ways to Work answers enquiries about jobsharing and flexible ways of working. It also provides a jobshare register.

The Working Mother's Association (WMA), 77 Holloway Road, London N1 8JZ, tel: 071-700 5771

The WMA has a network of local groups nationwide to discuss the options and problems of women at work.

National Childminding Association (NCA), 8 Masons Hill, Bromley, Kent BR2 9EY, tel: 081-464 6164

The NCA provides information on childminding.

Kids Clubs Network, 279-281 Whitechapel Road, E1 1BY, tel: 071-247 3009

Kids Clubs Network has details on after school and holiday schemes for children.

Working for a Charity (WFAC), 44-46 Caversham Road, London NW5 2DS, tel: 071-911 0353

WFAC runs three month preparatory courses which involve a mixture of training and work experience for those seeking a career in the charity sector. The programme has been designed with returners in mind.

Charity Action, 3 Down Place, Hammersmith W6 9JH

Charity Action places unemployed people, known as unwaged 'Actioneers', in work placements in charities for three days a week and provides free computer training. 'Actioneers', who contribute their skills, continue to receive benefits (income support, unemployment, housing, etc.) as well as lunch and travel expenses. The package offered helps people to find paid employment subsequently.

London Management Centre, University of Westminster, 35 Marylebone Road, London NW1 5LS, tel: 071-911 5000 ext.3061

The Centre runs a short course called 'Professional Updating for Women' for professional women who have taken a career break for various reasons and want to return to work.

The Directory of Social Change, Radius Works, Back Lane, London NW3 1HL, tel: 071-435 8171

DSC organises Charityfair, an annual event attended by many charities with various workshops, seminars and a Volunteering and Employment Forum, that include topics of interest to women returners. Held at the Business Design Centre in London during March.

> **"** *As a non-degree mother of two trying to establish a 'second career' – without any formal qualifications – I found experience counts for an awful lot. You just have to persevere and keep the contacts going. Let people know that you are available and be prepared to do mundane work enthusiastically and responsibly. As a volunteer – behave like a professional and it will pay off. And be flexible!* **"**
> Trisha Ward, Co-ordinator, Holocaust Survivors Centre

USEFUL PUBLICATIONS

Returning to Work, (London, 1993) from the National Council for One Parent Families, 255 Kentish Town Road, London NW5 2LX

Arrangements for Children, (London, 1993) from the National Council for One Parent Families

The Industrial Society has various publications available, including the Pepperell Department's *Resource Pack for Women Returners*.

8
AFTER REDUNDANCY: OPPORTUNITIES & OPTIONS

Redundancy is something which many people in the UK are having to face up to at one time or another. It can be a devastating experience. Yet, with positive help and support, it can become a turning point for positive change and new growth. Working in the voluntary sector, either as a volunteer or in a paid capacity, or as a volunteer as a first step to a paid job, may be one option.

The impact of being made redundant can depend very much on your age and career achievements. It is more likely to be a problem for those in mid-career and those close to retirement, than for those in their twenties.

Because it happens to so many people, redundancy no longer carries the stigma it used to. It can provide you with the opportunity to reassess your career prospects and to design a new career path that matches your skills and aspirations. For some people it has proved to be a blessing in disguise and one that might become apparent to you in retrospect.

Whatever the circumstances of your redundancy, it is probably safe to assume that you will have feelings about leaving a job which you may have done for many years. Give yourself time and space to come to terms with your emotions. Many people seek counselling and this can be very helpful. This may be offered by your former employer as part of an outplacement package or from a voluntary organisation or a private counsellor. Some people find volunteering helps them come to terms with the change.

REDUNDANCY NEAR RETIREMENT

You may see redundancy as an opportunity for early retirement. With your redundancy package, your future pension and perhaps declining family income needs (as children leave home), you may decide that you do not need a regular job or paid employment. You could work on a part time or, maybe, on a consultancy basis, and fill the rest of your time with activities of your own choice.

You may find volunteering a rewarding way of spending your new found leisure. Some people like to contribute their considerable experience to a charity while others relish the prospect of learning new skills e.g. computer/database skills, advice giving, running a charity shop, administration.

REDUNDANCY AT AN EARLIER POINT IN YOUR CAREER

You will probably have two objectives:

- to find another job
- to fill your time constructively while you are doing this.

If you are planning to find work with a charity, then these two objectives can come together through taking a volunteer job while looking for a paid one.

The volunteer job will give you:

- a better insight into the nature of the charity sector and its job opportunities
- enhanced skills and experience
- a range of contacts and possible networks
- an opportunity to show your commitment to the sector.

There is a further opportunity open to you if you have received some financial compensation as part of your redundancy. You may wish to invest some money as well as time and effort into your future. There are several possible ways of doing this:

- employing a career consultant to help you plan your next career steps

- investing in training. A number of specialist courses have been devised to improve the skills required for working with a charity (*see end of chapter*).

Another option is to ask for a transitional secondment to a charity as part of your leaving process. Many companies now provide this, and it is an excellent way of getting to know the voluntary sector.

> **"** I was made redundant from my job as a personal manager in a large chartered accountants practice. I still had about two months left of pay and I didn't want to just sit at home. So it was suggested that I go on an eight-week secondment. I thought it was a brilliant idea and made an appointment to go to ARC (the Action Resource Centre) the very next day. They asked me what I wanted from the secondment. I said I wanted
> - to gain an understanding of mental health in the community
> - hands-on experience of mental health groups
> - contact with academic workers in the field.
>
> They came up with the Mental Health Foundation. I've been there assessing the personnel situation in the organisation. I've come up with some very interesting findings which I shall be putting in a report. **"**
>
> Ann-Marie Hersh, secondee to the Mental Health Foundation

FINDING A JOB WITH A CHARITY

You should not approach the idea of working for a charity as a soft option. It is no easier a marketplace than the commercial or public sectors. Most charities, and certainly all the larger ones, approach staff recruitment on as professional a basis as a company or public body would. They are looking for competent people with the requisite skills.

In addition, charities also look for two other qualities:
- a commitment to the cause that the charity is working for
- an ability to work creatively with limited resources.

Most charities do not have the elaborate support systems and service departments that exist in many companies. Employees have to be flexible and be able to work creatively in overcoming problems. To this extent, working for a charity may be more demanding than working in other sectors.

The First Step

You will need to find the right charity for you – see *Chapters 2 and 3* for guidance on this. Remember that whatever you do undertake, it must be something that you have a commitment to.

These basic guidelines will help you decide on the best option for you:

- take time to evaluate your own needs, especially
  - financial e.g. could you afford to take a lower salary?
  - social e.g. could you work alone from home or do you want to work in an office with others?
  - aims/goals e.g. what do you want to achieve or contribute to in a wider sense?
- be realistic – take time to review your skills, knowledge and experience
- consider whether independent advice would help you define your skills and possibilities
- consider whether you could work for yourself – perhaps in a consultancy role.

" This secondment to the Mental Health Foundation has increased my confidence in the skills I've got. I've realised that I can be a consultant, I can run my own business. When I've finished here I'm going to set up a consultancy business offering human resources skills to charities. "
Ann-Marie Hersh, secondee to the Mental Health Foundation

Salaries and Benefits

Salaries in charities have risen over the past ten years, although they are not as high as in other sectors. At junior and middle levels, the salary gap is not as wide as it is at the senior level. For example, a fundraiser with one or two years of experience could earn £15,000-£25,000 a year. A director of a medium-sized charity could earn around £25,000-£30,000 a year.

Some salaries are considerably less and some are considerably more depending on the size, location and type of charity. Medical research charities make up the largest group, and because they have the largest incomes, they tend to pay some of the highest salaries.

Volunteering and Secondment

You may see a volunteer job as a bridge between no job and a paid job and as an opportunity to enhance your future employability. Or, you may see it as part of your portfolio of paid and volunteer tasks. Whatever your motives for volunteering, you should base what you do:

- on your interests – or what you would like to learn about
- on your skills and personal qualities
- on the time you realistically have available.

Bear the following points in mind:

- check whether you out-of-pocket expenses or other remuneration will be paid
- ask what opportunities there are for training and enhancing your skills
- ascertain what support you will be given and who you will report to
- check how your performance will be assessed
- ask for a job description if possible.

If you have some paid time on your hands before you leave your post, you might like to ask your employers to find a placement for you with a suitable charity. Many employers now offer this as part of their out-placement package.

Trusteeship

The managing committees of charities are composed of volunteers who take full legal responsibility for seeing that the charity operates properly and uses its resources effectively. They are known as trustees.

Many charities, particularly middle-sized and smaller ones, are looking for people willing to serve as trustees.

> **"** I worked for BP for thirteen years until I took voluntary redundancy six months ago. I started as an engineer and then joined their High Flier programme. I worked in Commercial negotiations, financial departments and as the administration manager of an oil refinery overseas. I ended up as a Human Resources analyst. It was a twelve hour day, seven days a week schedule.
>
> It gave me a broad range of valuable experience but in the end I wanted a change. I wanted to do something with more social value. I took voluntary redundancy because it was a generous package and I thought – this will force me to change. I am interested in working in the voluntary sector because I want to work for something I believe in and with people who also share the same ideals.
>
> I bring administrative and project management skills as well as influencing and networking skills. I believe those skills are transferable to the voluntary sector.
>
> I am on a three month volunteer placement with the British Diabetic Association doing two projects. One is to look at the possible sources of finance for European projects. The second is to review all the grant making trusts. There are lots of small donations and no clear focus. I am setting up a data base in order to target the most appropriate trusts.
>
> It is giving me the time and experience to make the transition from a large organisation with many services and support provided by the charity – where you have to learn to do many things by yourself. It's very stretching and incredibly rewarding. **"**
>
> Georgia Johnson, volunteer with British Diabetic Association

They want people who are concerned with the cause and who can bring fresh ideas and thinking. Other skills particularly in demand are:

- managerial experience
- legal or accountancy expertise
- PR or marketing experience
- ability to make contacts which could lead to greater success in fundraising.

If you are enthusiastic, experienced and able to put in volunteer time, then becoming a charity trustee may be an ideal way of contributing. The Trustee Register maintains a list of people willing to serve as trustees. Their address is: c/o Reed Charity Fund, 114 Peascod Street, Windsor, Berks SL4 1DN, tel: 0753-868277.

See also *Chapter 14 – Becoming a Trustee.*

SOURCES OF HELP AND INFORMATION

Publications

The Voluntary Agencies Directory (Bedford Square Press). A guide to around 2,000 national voluntary organisations.

The Directory of Volunteer and Employment Opportunities by Jan Brownfoot and Frances Wilks (Directory of Social Change). More than 500 charities looking for volunteers, with information also on how they recruit staff.

Charity (Charities Aid Foundation), *Third Sector* and *NGO Finance.* Specialist magazines to keep you in touch.

Specialist Recruitment Agencies

CR Charity Recruitment, 40 Rosebery Avenue, London EC1R 4RN, tel: 071-833 0770

Charity People, Suite 308, The Chandlery, 50 Westminster Bridge Road, London SE1 7QY, tel: 071-721 7585

Charity Appointments, 3 Spitals Yard, London E1 6AQ, tel: 071-247 4502

Training Courses

Working for a Charity, 44-46 Caversham Road, London NW5 2DS, tel: 071-911 0353

Directory of Social Change, Radius Works, Back Lane, London NW3 1HL, tel: 071-8171

Volunteering

REACH, 89 Southwark Street, London SE1 0HD, tel: 071-928 0452 (REACH places professional men and women in unpaid positions)

Community Service Volunteers (CSV), 237 Pentonville Road, London N1 9NJ, tel: 071-278 6601.

Volunteer Bureau (nearest one in your local telephone directory).

Charity Action, 3 Down Place, London W6 9JH. Charity Action places people who have been unemployed for more than six months in a charity for three days a week. All DSS benefits are still payable and travel and lunch expenses are available. Send a letter or CV to Penny Borg-Grech at the above address.

Trusteeship

Trustee Services Unit, NCVO (National Council for Voluntary Organisations, Regents Wharf, All Saints Street, London N1 9RL, tel: 071-713 6161.

The "*Effective Trustee*" range of publications:

- Vol.1 *Roles and Responsibilities*
- Vol.2 *Aims and Resources*
- Vol.3 *Getting the work done*

All are £8.95 each and are available from the **Directory of Social Change**, Radius Works, Back Lane, London NW3 1HL, tel: 071-435 8171.

9
AFTER RETIREMENT: OPPORTUNITIES & OPTIONS

Older people, particularly if they are no longer in paid work, are much in demand as volunteers by charities of all kinds. They have the time and they have the experience, whether just of life or of something more specific. And they may also have a relevant professional qualification.

As a volunteer, you have a whole new way of life available to you, at a time and a pace to suit your needs. Also, the right voluntary job could lead you into new paths, meeting different people and learning interesting things.

> **"** My advice to older people about volunteering is that it will broaden their horizons, stimulate them and keep them young. It will give them an interest in life. They'll make a much wider circle of friends and find new interests. **"**
>
> Alan Brown, RSVP (Retired and Senior Volunteer Programme) volunteer, Community Service Volunteers

WHY VOLUNTEER?

Motivation varies with each individual, but most older people volunteer for broadly the same reasons as younger people do. It is useful to look at your motivations, as they contain the key to finding satisfaction in your voluntary work. You may want to volunteer because:

- you want a meaningful activity to fill your time
- you have particular skills acquired during your working life

and would like to contribute them to the community in some way

- you support the cause and want to do something about it
- you would like to meet new people, perhaps be part of a group
- you would like to learn to do new things
- you want to respond to an invitation to help.

If you support the cause, or have been invited to help by a friend, then obviously you will know what charity or charities you might approach.

If your objective is to meet new people, then it is important to choose a voluntary job where you will be working with others. If you want to learn a new skill, you may consider a volunteer job where there is training attached. For example, the **Tate Gallery** offers a year long training course in the History of Art to its volunteer guides, many of whom are retired.

> *I came into the world of charities quite by chance. Having worked in banking for over 40 years, I was offered the opportunity to raise funds for, and to organise the finances of, Macclesfield Silk Heritage Museum, as a run up to retirement.*
>
> Geoffrey Lees, volunteer with BESO (British Executive Service Overseas)

WHY USE YOUR BUSINESS OR PROFESSIONAL SKILLS?

Many people, when they retire, want to do something completely different. Others, however, want to offer some of the skills they have acquired during their working life. Some of the benefits include:

- the ability to go on using professional and other skills and having these appreciated
- the chance to face stimulating challenges without the stress of the commercial world
- having a regular structure to your life
- the opportunity to be valued for yourself irrespective of age
- the chance to give altruistically.

Volunteering by retired executives and senior citizens can be of very significant help to a charity as it provides access to skills which could not otherwise be paid for.

> **"** I applied to REACH (Retired Executives Action Clearing House) for someone with marketing skills to help with my magazine for young people in care. Almost out of the blue I had a call from a REACH volunteer, a man who had run a department with a £2 billion turnover. I thought he was having me on until I met him. He diagnosed that the magazine was going down the drain but could be saved by having a different sort of structure. 'You need to be a charity,' he said, and he helped us do it. **"**
>
> Tory Laughland, Director and Editor, Who Cares?

RETIRED, REDUNDANT OR WHAT?

In the current economic climate, many people faced with redundancy may need to plan their future lives as if they had taken early retirement. (*Redundancy is covered in Chapter 8*). If you are suddenly in the position of having to make a major lifestyle change like this in your forties or fifties, and you have time on your hands, it could be used for volunteering.

As with all voluntary work, you will need to think through the following points:

- what sort of work you want to do
- what income you have available and how much you need to earn
- how much time you can realistically give voluntarily
- what skills you would like to use
- what training you would like to receive
- how long you are prepared to commit yourself for
- what your physical needs are (e.g. questions of access, visual or hearing impairment etc.).

If you have an adequate pension, perhaps topped up by a redundancy settlement, you may not need to earn money. If you are less fortunate, you may need to spend some time in paid work. It may be possible to work for a charity for part of your time. You may even feel that you can accept a salary which will top up your pension income rather than be paid the rate for the job.

Whether you are early retired or just retired, volunteering can help maintain your morale and make your leisure time more enjoyable. And it doesn't matter what age you are either. Most volunteer jobs – with the exception of overseas postings – are part-time, although if you want to volunteer full-time there are plenty of opportunities to do so.

" I became involved with voluntary work at the age of 55 following extensive surgery over a three year period. Voluntary work saved my reason! I assisted in forming a Life Support Scheme, taught reading to NACRO clients. I also joined BESO. In 1990/91 I spent six months in Pakistan on a housing project. Unable to pursue full-time work, and with a reduced pension, due to early retirement, I started a part-time business at the age of 65 as a Business Skills trainer which I do alongside my voluntary work."

Michael Lucas, BESO (British Executive Service Overseas) volunteer

What's Available?

Whatever your income needs and the time you have available, you are likely to be struck by the sheer size and variety of the voluntary sector. You will need to find something that interests you, involves your skills and talents and which is convenient to your home.

" A friend suggested RSVP (the Retired and Senior Volunteer Programme run by Community Service Volunteers). I read the literature, saw the Community Manager at Community Service Volunteers (CSV) and decided to become a volunteer co-ordinator for Hertfordshire. Our national RSVP has meetings and an Annual Conference. So we meet and discuss issues and are encouraged to go on. It is always hard work but it is a lot of fun, too."

Tigger Hewitt, volunteer organiser for RSVP (Retired and Senior Volunteer Programme), CSV

Most people do not want to travel far from their home to volunteer. Some, on other the hand, relish the thought of travelling and volunteering abroad in the developing world and eastern Europe. As long as you are fit and healthy you are never to old to volunteer, including going overseas.

> **"** I think very highly of BESO (British Executive Service Overseas). I have travelled to many parts of the world, including Asia, the Caribbean, Africa and the Middle East as a BESO volunteer. I have been retired for ten years but want to go on with my work advising on bee keeping and apiculture – honey can be very important for developing countries. I have appreciated going overseas for BESO and have every intention of carrying on. If you come across something that needs doing and you can do it and you don't need to be paid for it, then going overseas is a different way of doing voluntary work. All you need is the initiative to get on and do it. **"**
> Dr Eva Crane, BESO (British Executive Service Overseas) volunteer

CHECKLIST TO CONSIDER

Once you have decided what organisation you want to work for and have been accepted, there are some points to consider:
- what your job will be, what your responsibilities will be and who you will report to
- what support services you will be able to call on (e.g. clerical or secretarial)
- how much time will be involved
- whether your out-of-pocket expenses will be met
- whether training and support are available
- if there is insurance cover (if relevant).

INDUCTION AND TRAINING

Ask if there is an induction process so that you can see how the organisation works and how you can best fit in. If there is no formal procedure, you may want to ask to be shown around, to meet and talk to staff and other volunteers. It is a good idea to obtain a copy of the organisation's Annual Report and other relevant literature.

Many voluntary organisations offer training. Sometimes it is on-the-job training. Sometimes it is more specialised training, e.g. for counselling work. And often, there are opportunities to acquire new hands-on skills such as word-processing. If you feel that, as a volunteer, your skills and performance would be enhanced through training, then ask about opportunities.

“ *I started working with REACH about fifteen months ago on a project to establish a nationwide service speaking directly to companies who have pre-retirement programmes. I organise a team of fourteen volunteers all over the country who go and talk about the options for voluntary work.*

I retired early. I was Chief Executive of the Road Transport Industrial Training Board. My specific background was organising training courses as well as interfacing with the public and private sectors. It's much the same kind of work in my placement with REACH. I deal with companies in a variety of industries. I feel that now I have the best bits, without the hassle of my previous job.

All my expertise goes into my voluntary work. I didn't set out to do it – it just happened. I was prepared to tackle anything. We are very fortunate to have such a well-organised infra-structure to enable people to volunteer. We have such an enormous resource in our people in this country.

I get a good deal of quiet satisfaction in all sorts of ways. I am in touch with people in the professional context that I've been used to. Of course, none of this is meaningful unless you're in a situation of reasonable financial security. If that's not the case, then you have to think of other priorities.

My advice to anyone is – don't volunteer because you think you ought. Only do it for fun. Don't do it for it's own sake. If you can't get a glow of satisfaction from it then leave it alone. I get a tremendous sense of achievement and fun out of it. It gives me a chance to make my life in retirement more meaningful and also to carry on using the skills that I acquired in my professional working life. **”**

David Barnett, REACH (Retired Executives Action Clearing House) volunteer

How to Find the Right Volunteer Job

There are several organisations set up to help intending volunteers find just the right slot for their individual circumstances.

Volunteer Bureaux

The 300+ Volunteer Bureaux promote volunteering of all kinds. They maintain a register of local charities that are looking for people to help with specific projects. Contact your local Bureau direct (number in your local telephone book).

RSVP (Retired and Senior Volunteer Programme)

Mainly concerned with setting up local projects where groups of older people with a variety of skills and experience come together to carry out a specific task for the benefit of the local community. A central body, supervising 55 area organisers, it helps with co-ordination and identification of needs. Contact RSVP, Community Service Volunteers, 237 Pentonville Road, London N1 9NJ, tel: 071-278 6601.

REACH (Retired Executives Action Clearing House)

Recruits and places people with business or professional expertise in part-time, expenses only voluntary jobs with charities who need, but can't afford, their particular experience. Apart from the usual business disciplines of general management, finance, marketing and personnel, REACH volunteers have had experience in such fields as: education; law; the Civil Service; engineering; medicine; training; and journalism. This free job-finding service is available throughout Britain. Contact REACH at 89 Southwark Street, London SE1 0HD, tel: 071-928 0452.

BESO (British Executive Service Overseas)

Sets up short term (two weeks to six months) advisory and training projects in overseas and developing countries (including Eastern Europe). Maintains a register of qualified specialists who are available to work as unpaid volunteers, with travel and other expenses paid, including those of a partner, as projects are identified. Contact BESO at 164 Vauxhall Bridge Road, London SW1V 2RB, tel: 071-630 0644.

VSO (Voluntary Service Overseas)

Concerned with arranging longer term (two years minimum) assignments for people who wish to gain experience overseas. Contact VSO at 317 Putney Bridge Road, London SW15 2PG, tel: 081-780 2266.

Volunteer Centre UK

Promotes volunteering of all kinds, including offering an information service which, whilst not arranging jobs directly, provides classified lists of charities which may need volunteers. Contact the Volunteer Centre UK, 29 Lower King's Road, Berkhamsted, Herts, tel: 0442-873311.

SCORE (The Scottish Corps of Retired Executives)

Maintains a register of retired professionals who are willing to be assigned as volunteers to carry out tasks for charities in various parts of Scotland. Contact Scottish Business in the Community, Romano House, 43 Station Road, Edinburgh EH12 7AF, tel: 031-334 9876.

Other agencies which may be of use:

Wales Council for Voluntary Action, Lyls Ifor, Crescent Road, Caerphilly, Wales CF8 1XL, Tel: 02222-869224

Volunteer Development Scotland, 80 Murray Place, Stirling, Scotland SK8 2BX, Tel: 0786-479593.

USEFUL BOOKS AND PUBLICATIONS

Good Deeds in Old Age: Volunteering by the New Leisured Class by Susan Maizell (published by Lexington Books, USA)

Directory of Volunteer and Employment Opportunities by Jan Brownfoot and Frances Wilks (published by the Directory of Social Change)

Prospects – Scotland's Action and Opportunities Package for Older People (published by Scottish Community Education Guidance)

The **Volunteer Centre UK** publishes various information sheets including: *'Finding out about Volunteering in your area'*, *'Volunteering Opportunities UK'* and *'Volunteering Opportunities Overseas'*.

10
WORKING AND VOLUNTEERING OVERSEAS

Working and volunteering overseas present both challenges and potential personal gains. There are often unaccustomed inconveniences, uncomfortable circumstances and even dangers to be faced. Despite these potential difficulties, volunteers frequently return with increased confidence, new friends, a greater understanding of the world and a renewed sense of purpose and motivation. Many describe it as 'the best experience' of their lives.

> **"** I wanted to see another country and another culture. I picked Indonesia because the project offered work in a university as a teacher's aid, and it sounded quite exotic. One of the biggest problems was coping with the heat. There was also the problem of culture shock and feelings of homesickness to deal with. But I feel I came back stronger and more mature. Everything I did had to be my decision and my choice. I couldn't rely on anybody else. There were so many things I'd never seen or experienced before. You go out so naive and young, and realise there is very much more to learn in life. I've learnt a great deal about myself and a little bit about the world also. **"**
>
> Anna Heffron, GAP volunteer in Indonesia

> **"** I had lived in one area all my life with my parents looking after me generally. So it was great for me going out to Australia and seeing the country. It was good experience looking after yourself and fending for yourself. I spent time working in the Outback. That takes you back to basics because there is no entertainment, so you have to make your own. I came home more self confident because of all this and of getting to know strangers. 'Go travelling and discover yourself' – that's what I did. **"**
>
> Tom Hopewell, GAP volunteer in Australia

A period of working overseas as a volunteer, whether in a paid or unpaid capacity, can be greatly rewarding and have mutual benefits for those volunteering and for the people they go to work with. Opportunities have grown considerably in recent years. Whether you are a school leaver or taking early retirement, a recent graduate or a skilled, experienced professional, taking a year out or unemployed, you will find various possibilities exist to work on projects in both developed and developing countries, short-term (e.g. three months) or longer-term (e.g. three years).

WHY DO YOU WANT TO GO OVERSEAS?

Before applying to volunteer overseas you need to think carefully about what such work involves and why you want to do it. In recent years there have been many changes in attitudes and approach to the non-Western world. For example, the term 'Third World' is less used now, compared with 'developing world' or 'The South'.

It is also inappropriate to think that you are going to 'help' countries which are 'undeveloped'. The reasons why many countries in the world today are struggling with poverty, malnutrition, illiteracy, poor housing, economic problems and discrimination, are very complex. They include historical factors such as colonialism, as well as the effects of climate, possibly limited natural resources and unequal trading practices.

Don't forget also that many Western countries are today facing similar problems to those of developing areas, including the effects of civil war and socio-economic disruption. Agencies which send volunteers overseas from Britain now expect that those going will be working with people in the host country on an equal basis.

So, ask yourself *'why do I want to volunteer overseas?'* and *'what do I hope to gain from it?'* It may be that you:

- want to take a year off between school and further education
- need to gain some relevant experience for a particular type of career e.g. the environment, teaching
- are unemployed
- want to contribute specialist skills
- are committed to social change and the cause of peace and justice globally
- feel a religious or other commitment to 'do something'

Working overseas is not an easy alternative to finding employment at home. You will need various personal skills and strengths and the ability to adapt to circumstances very different from those you are used to. You have only to think of the pictures you see on television of communities torn apart by civil war, of the sick and the maimed, and of the squalor of refugee camps, to realise some of the conditions in which aid organisations and volunteers work overseas. These include countries as diverse as the former Yugoslavia, Somalia and Iraq.

Ask yourself:

- Can I accept and work with people from different ethnic, cultural and religious backgrounds?
- Am I willing to learn from those I work among?
- Can I cope with different living conditions/food/climate/accommodation/standards of hygiene and health care?
- What about homesickness or ill health? – contracting malaria, diarrhoea, dysentery, hepatitis are all possibilities
- How will I manage with the language? – am I able to learn Japanese/Indonesian/Pushtu/Spanish/whatever?
- If I am one of very few expatriates, perhaps the only one, will I be able to cope with isolation?
- Can I live on a limited maintenance allowance?

Once you have considered all the pros and cons, weighed up the disadvantages as well as the many advantages of working overseas, you can then decide objectively whether you really want to go. If the answer is 'Yes', you will then need to consider whether to go for a short or longer period, obviously depending on your individual circumstances and the time you have available.

> **❝** I have always had the urge to work in a remote, far-flung corner of the globe. Also to help, in however small a way, with environmental and community projects, such as assisting with rain forest research and helping to provide educational facilities in remote areas. There was also the satisfaction of surviving the physical challenges of expedition life. I never thought I would be able to cope with sleeping in the jungle, just under a tarpaulin cover and a mosquito net! I now know what it is like living in basic conditions and with very little. I have never appreciated a shower so much, even a cold one!**❞**
>
> Kate Crane, formerly a volunteer Travel Officer with Raleigh International

LONG-TERM OPPORTUNITIES

Most long-term working/volunteering opportunities overseas are for skilled, qualified and experienced people prepared to work on extended placements in developing countries.

Volunteer-sending agencies in the UK are working towards lasting and sustainable development by responding to requests for overseas workers from individual countries. By sharing skills with people and communities in the developing world volunteers can help to build independence and self-reliance in the countries where they work.

Many of the jobs involve the volunteers in teaching or training local people, thus ensuring that skills are not lost when they leave. Volunteers invariably return home with a sense of having learned as much as they have taught. A great many continue to participate in wider efforts to inform and stimulate public opinion on development issues at home.

You will need:

- to be qualified and experienced in your field
- have a commitment to working for social and economic change overseas.

Age restrictions vary from agency to agency but applicants must generally be between 21 and 65, although there are short-term schemes for school leavers and gap years.

Common requests are for workers in:

- education
- agriculture and natural resources

- health
- business
- social development
- technical projects.

Conditions of employment vary from agency to agency. But in general:

- posts are usually for two years, although some may be for a shorter period
- language and orientation training are given
- salaries are based on local pay
- accommodation is provided
- return air-fares are paid
- medical insurance is covered
- National Insurance (NI) contributions or equivalent are paid
- pre-departure, mid-term and re-settlement grants are available.

ORGANISATIONS TO CONTACT

Voluntary Service Overseas (VSO)

is probably the best known volunteer sending agency. In 1993 VSO had over 1,500 men and women, aged from 20 to 70, working in 50 different countries in Africa, Asia, the Caribbean and the Pacific.

VSO's stated purpose is to enable British men and women to work alongside people in poorer countries in order to share skills, build capabilities and promote international understanding and action, in the pursuit of a more equitable world.

VSO invests in people. It gives priority to posts that cannot be filled locally. VSO jobs overseas usually require a two-year commitment to ensure that skills are passed on effectively. This period of time also enables the development of real understanding on both sides. VSO selects volunteers on the basis of their skills, experience and suitability for the range of jobs available, and prefers them to be flexible about which country they are posted to.

Since VSO responds to requests for volunteers from employers overseas, the range of skills in demand is very wide, although most fall into the areas of education, health, natural resources, engineering, technical trades, business or social development. Most VSO volunteers need a professional or trade qualification and over 18 months relevant work experience in their field. However, VSO can place newly trained teachers, and there are some opportunities for recent graduates in teaching posts where the degree is relevant to the teaching subject requested.

> **"** Working with the Ni-Vanuatu is both a pleasure and an education. The work is co-operative...There are of course moments when conditions in the field are arduous...But even when things are at their worst I rarely lose sight of what a complete and fulfilling experience it is. **"**
> Jos Wheatley, VSO botanist in Vanuatu

Some volunteers are able to get leave of absence if already in employment. VSO also provides those going overseas with training courses, country and medical briefings, and names of returned volunteers. Assistance is also available to volunteers to help them find jobs after their return to the UK.

> **"** Two hours by bus and then ten by foot to Shiva Laai. Young district midwives Apsara and Ramperi, Kabi our porter and I were to spend the next several weeks going to distant health posts to run midwifery courses for village women.... With their help, the chance to hand over health information to the village women of this mid-mountain region of Nepal was my privilege and pleasure. **"**
> Maureen Minden, VSO health worker in Nepal

The aim of every VSO project is to help people help themselves. VSO believes in countering disadvantage by practical action, person to person, and values and respects diversity of culture. It emphasises action motivated by and responding to the needs of others, and the learning and friendship which result from people living and working alongside each other in the pursuit of shared goals.

> **"** I work for the Yankari Initiative which aims to help the State Wildlife Service conserve this particularly beautiful part of Nigeria and the wildlife in it. I aim to train Abdullahi, the trainee mechanic to replace me when I leave in 1994.**"**
>
> Andy Hawson, VSO mechanic in Nigeria

> **"** My first task was to gain the confidence of the local Khmer people....Learning the language was difficult but worthwhile. Now I am able to communicate with my colleagues, wheel and deal with local traders and negotiate tenders with contractors. The rewards of my job are immense.**"**
>
> Paul Toal, VSO site supervisor, Cambodia

Other Volunteer-Sending Organisations

The **Overseas Development Administration** (ODA) supports four independent voluntary agencies that send overseas suitably qualified, skilled volunteers, usually with work experience, in response to requests from developing countries. They are:

- **International Cooperation for Development** (ICD), part of the Catholic Institute for International Relations (CIIR) – recruits volunteers particularly for community projects to promote the interests of the poor
- **Skillshare Africa** – sends skilled people to four southern African countries
- **United Nations Association International Service** (UNAIS) – works for friendship and understanding, and sends volunteers mainly to agricultural, health and social development projects
- **Voluntary Service Overseas** (VSO) – including its East European Partnership (EEP) (a special unit of VSO set up in 1990) which recruits teachers and nurses to work in various countries in Eastern Europe.

The **ODA Joint Funding Scheme** (JFS) also supports hundreds of long-term projects run by over 100 British Non-Governmental Organisations (NGOs) in various developing countries. These NGOs include **Action Aid**, the **British Red**

Cross and **Womankind Worldwide**. The majority do not employ volunteers but may recruit experienced, qualified staff to work on their projects in the field.

Christian Organisations

If you have a Christian commitment there are various organisations which welcome skilled workers including:

- **Christians Abroad**
- **Tear Fund**
- **Christian Outreach**
- **Volunteer Missionary Movement** (VMM).

Agencies in other Countries

Many other countries also have their own national volunteer sending agencies. Some of these include:

- **The Agency for Personal Service Overseas** (APSO) in Eire
- **Canadian University Service Overseas** (CUSO) in Ottawa
- **Overseas Service Bureau** in Melbourne, Australia

The **United Nations Volunteers** (UNV) in Geneva is an international agency with over 2,000 skilled volunteers working in 100 developing countries. UNV can accept applications from couples with up to two children and volunteers from all member countries of the United Nations are eligible. Information and application forms for UNV are available from VSO.

SHORT-TERM OPPORTUNITIES

So what possibilities are there for working overseas for periods of anything up to a year? You will find a number of organisations offering shorter term volunteering opportunities. These are frequently for younger people. Many include a requirement to fundraise towards the cost of sending you. The commitment to raise the money and the actual fundraising process are seen as an essential part of the volunteering experience. Some people find that going on such a project opens up possibilities for paid work with the sending organisation after their return to the UK.

Raleigh International, Health Projects Abroad, Project Trust and **Gap Activity Projects** are examples of these types of scheme.

A 'Gap' Year

Many of these projects offer opportunities for young people wanting to take a year off between school and further education, starting full-time work or building a career. More opportunities now exist to do this than ever before. Often called a *Gap Year*, such time gives you an invaluable opportunity to assess yourself, what you want to do in life, and where your strengths and weaknesses lie. It is a vitally important part of an individual's personal development.

Many young people use their gap year to volunteer abroad. In doing so they become far more self confident and mature, as well as developing personal and practical skills. Placements include work experience, the opportunity to acquire new skills, growth in awareness of the problems faced by other communities and cultures, and the satisfaction of making a useful contribution in another part of the world. There is also the enrichment and enjoyment that come from learning about another country and its people. Colleges and employers now generally recognise and endorse the value of taking a year off, providing you use it effectively and don't lie around watching television!

> **❝** It's definitely worth taking a gap year when you do something worthwhile. I've benefited from the fact of seeing somewhere so different. There is education on both sides. At a basic level we improved the Pathan children's English and gave them a more objective view of what the West is like. Also you can correct wrong images in the UK when you get back.
>
> Going overseas has given me an education and an insight – into another major world religion, Islam, and into Pakistan, Afghanistan and the refugee situation. It's helped to build my self confidence and given me a feeling of achievement. It's also given me more direction in life. I'd very much like to work abroad after university. Going overseas on a gap year opens your eyes and gives you more tolerance. **❞**
>
> Jeremy Weston, former gap year volunteer in Pakistan with the Project Trust

> **“** I went with three other GAP volunteers and worked in Japan in two Cheshire Homes mainly for people with cerebral palsy. We were living and working in a Japanese environment so we had to start learning the language. The Japanese staff were sympathetic and treated us so well. They were wonderful. I would recommend to other young people to take a chance and do a gap year because it is so rewarding and you learn so much. I learnt independence, tolerance, and how to survive in a foreign land and culture on your own. I've become friends with various Japanese people and I keep in touch with the Homes. It has broadened my horizons and perspectives on everything. I really thank GAP that they gave me the place. **”**
> Emily Richmond, volunteer with GAP in Japan

GAP Activity Projects

GAP Activity Projects, a registered educational charity, organises project and work opportunities for young people who want to volunteer overseas, before moving on to higher education. The aim is to enable young people to learn about other countries and also make a contribution to international understanding. GAP arranges placements in around 30 different countries mainly in Asia, Europe and North and South America.

The placements organised are not paid jobs but are with employers who need volunteers and can provide board and lodging, pastoral care and pocket money. The kind of work includes:

- teaching English as a foreign language
- assisting in schools and colleges of all kinds
- office work
- caring for the sick, handicapped and deprived
- conservation
- farming.

Placements usually last between six and nine months, with opportunities to travel afterwards. Apart from a registration fee on application, if selected each volunteer has to pay for various costs including an administration fee, the return air fare, medical expenses and spending money. Each is encouraged to earn the amount required or find sponsors. Depending on the type and location of the project, costs can vary from a few hundred pounds to £2,000 or more.

> **"** I had to raise nearly £600 to go to Slovakia. Friends and neighbours helped, and Rotary, various companies and a local Trust sponsored me. I did a one week TEFL (Teaching English as a Foreign Language) course and then taught employees of a copyright lawyer's agency in Bratislava. I was thrown in at the deep end. There weren't many other English speakers around. I had to find the resources and decide the methods of teaching myself. My students were very eager to learn and were extremely receptive, and their English improved a good deal.
>
> The gap year was a very worthwhile thing to do. You are working to benefit other people and be of service, and to benefit yourself by meeting people and experiencing a different culture first-hand. My confidence has increased too. My GAP project was the most worthwhile thing I've ever done. **"**
>
> Simon Goodfellow, GAP volunteer in Slovakia

> **"** I raised the complete £2,500 myself. I approached trusts and a local company, and also Rotary and Round Table. Friends gave some. I worked myself waitressing, and used my own savings too. In Indonesia I worked with another GAP volunteer, Cath Disher, in a university in Sulawesi. We went as teacher's assistants but were regarded as fully qualified English teachers! We were teaching from two text books, one English and one American. A lot of the material wasn't relevant so we had to improvise and make up our own lessons. We were teaching people aged from 20 to about 55.
>
> Going to Indonesia was the most frightening thing I've ever done. You go with a sense of idealism and enthusiasm and think you're going to achieve so much. And then you realise you can't change the world, but can only try to help it. You have to have an open mind and be flexible and adaptable to make it work. **"**
>
> Anna Heffron, GAP volunteer to Indonesia

> **❝** *I worked on conservation projects in Australia with the Australian Trust for Conservation Volunteers (ATCV). It included removing noxious weeds, fencing, seed collecting and doing a tour of schools in isolated areas talking to children about England and conservation.*
>
> *It was all communal living, including camping out and learning to make do. You have to get used to talking to, and meeting, people.*
>
> *It was really worthwhile to take a year off. I would say to anybody 'definitely go – with your eyes wide open!.* **❞**
>
> Tom Hopewell, GAP volunteer to Australia

Project Trust

Founded in 1967 and now over 25 years old, Project Trust is an educational trust specialising in placing young people in overseas projects for a year between school and higher education. The aim is to give them a better understanding of the world through structured experience, as well as travel, in a specific project and country.

Projects fall into three main areas: Teacher-Aides, Social Services and Outdoor Activities. They include:

- English language teaching in schools and universities
- running sports and clubs in schools
- working in children's homes and hospitals
- assisting in health and community development projects
- farming

The work has to be satisfying to the volunteer and useful to the host organisation. Selection includes interviews and a 4-day course at Project Trust's Ballyhough Centre on the Isle of Coll. Training courses are provided before departure, together with support in the field as necessary. Volunteers have to find nearly £3,000 towards total costs by raising it from trusts, donors, sponsorship and other methods, with assistance from Project Trust.

A year overseas provides long-term job experience which can help improve career prospects, invaluable personal development, enhanced understanding of another community and a sense of sharing skills and abilities with others, while developing self reliance and responsibility. Project Trust volunteers are de-briefed fully following their return to the UK.

> " I knew about Project Trust from my sister who had volunteered. I wanted to volunteer for a whole year, not for a shorter period. I raised the money from charitable trusts, sponsored events like a 100 mile bike ride, donations, and family and friends. I got a lot of help from my school too. I was placed in a new project in Pakistan, in the Swat Valley, with one other volunteer.
>
> We taught English as a second language in a school for children. All the other subjects were in Pushtu. I taught children aged from four to nine, mostly boys, using books and a blackboard. I really enjoyed it and really benefited from being able to see the different cultures. A lot of the magic of the place was the people – the Pathans and their hospitality. And they too were able to meet people from somewhere else, as few tourists go there.
>
> We lived in a room in the school and cooked for ourselves or went out. We both got amoebic dysentery. At first I was concerned when I got ill. But then I was glad, in a way, that it happened because it was all part of the year's experience and we learnt to take ill health in our stride. "
>
> Jeremy Weston, former gap year volunteer in Pakistan with the Project Trust

Raleigh International

Raleigh International is a charity which aims to develop young people by giving them the opportunity to carry out demanding environmental and community projects in the UK and around the world.

Raleigh offers a rare chance to make a valuable contribution in remote and unfamiliar parts of the world, with lasting benefits for host countries' communities, the environment, conservation and scientific research. Raleigh expeditions are ten weeks long, with some five week ones planned for 1994, and go to such countries as Guyana, Chile, Namibia, Zimbabwe, Malaysia and Russia.

Since being launched as Operation Raleigh in 1984 – re-launched as Raleigh International in 1992 – over 8,000 young people aged between 17 and 25, and called 'Venturers', have taken part in the programme. An expedition offers an unparalleled opportunity for personal achievement and advancement which is open to all, regardless of background, formal qualifications and financial resources. Each Venturer has an individual fund-raising target of anything between £500 and £3,000 according to circumstances. Following their return to the UK they link in with any one of 42 support groups and carry on doing voluntary work in their home communities.

Every year Raleigh also recruits 350 volunteer members of staff from the UK to work on expeditions with local people in each country. These staff, aged 26 and over, usually have special skills, such as being engineers or medics, and are often sponsored to go by their employer in the UK.

" I decided to explore working for a non-profit making organisation whose aims were to help others rather than generate money. There was also the challenge of working with limited resources in a totally different environment, and further developing my marketing skills. I submitted an application form to Raleigh and was called for an interview for the Travel Officer post for an expedition to Malaysia. I was prepared to leave immediately.

I had sole responsibility for all air and bus travel on the expedition, as well as providing general administrative and support functions, such as purchasing supplies for project sites. Having done the job, I now feel so much more confident in areas which used to fill me with dread, such as travelling to unknown places and being with people I had never met before.

The work we carried out on the expedition included collecting sponges for cancer treatment, monitoring wildlife in the rain forest, and constructing bridges and buildings. There were also many intangible benefits such as showing how young people from many different backgrounds and parts of the world can work together constructively.

On returning to the UK I was asked to work for Raleigh International's Commercial Division on a freelance basis. The role involves design and photography, and is invaluable experience in publicity work for a voluntary organisation, an area I now wish to specialise in. There is a high level of motivation too – people at Raleigh are very positive and energetic."

Kate Crane, formerly part-time Design & Picture Library Co-ordinator, Raleigh International

International Work Camps

International work camps, which run for two to four weeks and sometimes longer, provide another opportunity for working overseas and giving community service. The United Nations Association (UNA) and International Voluntary Service (IVS) are among the organisations that set up work camps.

Types of work include:
- community
- conservation/environmental
- building/construction
- gardening
- decorating

BESO (British Executive Service Overseas)

If you are an older person then you may find BESO is a more appropriate organisation.

BESO sends experienced, often retired, volunteers with business, professional and technical skills to provide assistance to private and public organisations in developing countries. To 1993 over 2,000 projects had been undertaken.

In addition, BESO is seeing a dramatic rise in the number of requests for assistance from countries in East and Central Europe and the former Soviet Union. With over 120 assignments completed since 1991 and another 51 in the pipeline (mid-1993), BESO's high profile continues to increase awareness of British industry in countries where a burgeoning free market economy is struggling to establish itself.

> *"One afternoon BESO rang to ask me whether I would be interested in an assignment in Guyana (South America) to re-organise the administration of the National Bank of Industry and Commerce. I readily accepted. Out of the staff of 330, I had the unique experience of being an ethnic minority of one. We all got on like old friends. Although I was introducing radical new systems, I had the enthusiastic support of the staff which made the job easy. I received enormous job satisfaction because the impact I was making was far greater than my doing the same job in Britain."*
>
> Geoffrey Lees, retired banker and BESO volunteer

> "I retired in 1983. Since then I have been going overseas to Asia, Africa and the Caribbean for BESO on projects to do with bee keeping and honey production. I have visited many different countries and projects. In Uganda they do their honey harvesting after dark, so while I was there I went with the bee-keepers into the mountains by night. In Vietnam we had to go by wooden dug-out canoe into the swamps of the Mekong delta to get to where the bees were. In Pakistan I went to help commercial bee-keepers in the North West Frontier Province. One, was such a strict Moslem that he wouldn't look at me at all.
>
> I don't go on these trips thinking 'I must do this and this and this'. I listen first so that I can find out what they are doing and what their problems are, and so that I can praise them too. I learn more than I teach I'm sure. But the people I'm with think I can help them, and I can. I'm a channel through to the wider world for them and, if nothing else, I can put them in touch with people who can help.
>
> I go to out-of-the-way countries and often I don't see another European from the moment I arrive until I get on the plane to come back. I try to stay down-market and to live among the local people.
>
> I really enjoy it. It's so stimulating. You can see that you are needed and that you can do something useful."
>
> Dr Eva Crane, retired bee specialist and BESO *volunteer*

USEFUL ORGANISATIONS AND ADDRESSES

ABM, Church House, Great Smith Street, London SW1P 3NZ, tel: 071-222 9011

BESO, 164 Vauxhall Bridge Road, London SW1V 2RB, tel: 071-630 0644

British Trust for Conservation Volunteers, 36 St Mary's Street, Wallingford, Oxon OX10 0EU, tel: 0491-39766

Christian Outreach, 1 New Street, Leamington Spa CV31 1HP, tel: 0926-315301

Christians Abroad, 1 Stockwell Green, London SW9 9HP, tel: 071-737 7811

CIT, 7b Broad Street, Nottingham NG1 3AJ, tel: 0602-470906

Concordia (Youth Service Volunteers), 8 Brunswick Place, Hove, Sussex BN3 1ET, tel: 0273-772086

Council of Churches for Britain and Ireland, Youth Matters, 35-41 Lower Marsh, London SE1 7RL, tel: 071-620 4444

Eastern European Partnership (EEP), 15 Princeton Court, Felsham Road, London SW15 1AZ, tel: 081-780 2841

GAP Activity Projects, Gap House, 44 Queens Road, Reading RG1 4BB, tel: 0734-594914

Health Projects Abroad, HMS President, Victoria Embankment, London EC4 0HJ, tel: 071-583 5725

Health Unlimited, 3 Stamford Street, London SE1 9NT, tel: 071-928 8105

International Cooperation for Development (ICD), Unit 3, Canonbury Yard, 190a New North Road, London N1 7BJ, tel: 071-354 0883

International Voluntary Service (IVS), Old Hall, East Bergholt, Colchester CO7 6TQ

Kibbutz Representatives, 1a Accommodation Road, London NW11, tel: 081-458 9235

Missions to Seamen, Ministry Secretary, St Michael Paternoster Royal, College Hill, London EC4R 2RL, tel: 071-248 7442

Project Trust, The Hebridean Centre, Ballyhough, Isle of Coll, Argyll PA78 6TE, tel: 087-93 444

Quaker International Social Projects (QISP), Quaker Social Responsibility and Education, Friends House, 173-177 Euston Road, London NW1 2BJ, tel: 071-387 3601

Raleigh International, Raleigh House, 27 Parsons Green Lane, London SW6 4HS, tel: 071-371 8585

Romania Orphanage Trust, PO Box 999, Bridport, Dorset DT6 5YD, tel: 0308-27356

Skillshare Africa, 3 Belvoir Street, Leicester LE1 6SL, tel: 0533-541862

Tear Fund, 100 Church Road, Teddington, Middlesex TW11 8QE, tel: 081-977 9144

Third World First, 232 Cowley Road, Oxford OX4 1HU, tel: 0865-245678

UNA (Wales) International Youth Service, The Welsh Centre for International Affairs, Temple of Peace, Cathays Park, Cardiff, Wales, tel: 0222-223088

UNAIS, Suite 3A, Hunter House, 57 Goodramgate, York YO1 2LS, tel: 0904-647799

United Nations Volunteers (UNV), Palais des Nations, 1211 Geneva 10, Switzerland, tel: 010 41 22-7985850

VMM, Comboni House, London Road, Sunningdale SL5 0JY, tel: 0344-875380

USEFUL INFORMATION AND PUBLICATIONS

Third World Directory, edited by Lucy Stubbs (published by Directory of Social Change)

The International Directory of Voluntary Work (Vacation Work Publications)

Kibbutz Volunteer (Vacation Work Publications)

Volunteer Work (Central Bureau for Educational Visits and Exchanges, 5th edition 1992)

A Year Between (Central Bureau)

Working Holidays (Central Bureau)

A Year Off...A Year On? (Hobson's Publishing)

Go for It! Martyn Lewis's Essential Guide to Opportunities for Young People by Martyn Lewis (Lennard Publishing, 1993)

Volunteering Opportunities – Overseas (The Volunteer Centre UK, 1992)

Volunteering in Europe: Opportunities and Challenges in the 90s, edited by Justin Davis Smith (The Volunteer Centre UK, 1993)

International Jobs A Guide for UK and Overseas Students (University of London Careers Advisory Service, 1991)

The **Central Bureau for Educational Visits and Exchanges**, which is in Seymour Mews, London W1 9PE, tel: 071-486 5101 and has offices in Edinburgh and Belfast, can provide advice and information, as well as various publications and leaflets.

11
GUIDELINES & OPPORTUNITIES FOR PEOPLE WITH DISABILITIES

There are approximately 500,000 charities and voluntary organisations in the UK covering everything from the developing world to medical research, children and animal welfare. Among them are organisations working specifically for and with people with disabilities. Some of these have been set up, and are often completely run, by disabled people.

The voluntary sector needs and uses volunteers and paid employees in a variety of roles. The professional skills that voluntary organisations require are similar to those needed in commercial organisations, although some, such as counselling and advice-giving, fundraising and campaigning, are more specialised. Disabled people have, or can develop, skills and abilities that voluntary organisations can and do use, both as paid employees and as volunteers. They should be encouraged in these roles. If you have a disability, this chapter provides you with guidance on the laws, services and organisations that exist to help you, as well as illustrating the kinds of opportunities available.

The Charity Culture

Charities of various kinds exist to work for people with disabilities. The work involved might be providing a service or it might be campaigning or lobbying to change attitudes or practice. The types of disabilities that voluntary organisations cover include the whole range of mental and physical disablement, everything from learning difficulties and head injuries to arthritis and blindness. A disability can be genetic, such as cystic fibrosis, or acquired, such as through a serious accident. It can be visible, as with someone who uses a wheelchair, or is blind, or hidden, as with someone who has dyslexia or depression.

Some of the organisations in this field are self-help organisations mobilising the energies and skills of those with disabilities themselves. Others work for people with disabilities and may or may not use such people as staff or volunteers.

Many people think that having a disability means inability. But numerous people have disabilities that have no practical impact on them undertaking work. If there are practical barriers they can frequently be overcome, usually by straightforward solutions such as better lighting, providing a dictaphone or offering flexible working hours. The most serious barriers to disabled people working are often the invisible ones – convincing both potential employers and people with a disability that they have abilities.

Like the voluntary sector as a whole, in recent years the range and numbers of voluntary organisations addressing disability have grown. However, some of the most well known, or largest, charities were set up years ago, often by concerned groups of people, typically parents, who wanted to do something to help those people suffering from a certain kind of disability. As a result, many focus on a specific condition and target people with this condition, for example, the **Spastics Society**, **Mencap** and the **Spinal Injuries Association**.

Most of these charities are not controlled or managed by people with disabilities – the Spastics Society and Mencap are not disability-led organisations, although the Spinal Injuries Association is. In recent years there has been a growing movement to empower people with disabilities by enabling them to play active and positive roles in the organisations which exist for them. People with disabilities have also set up charities themselves, many of them largely, if not fully, staffed by disabled people.

Due to rigorous campaigning by such disability-led groups, many charities in other areas of work are positively encouraging people with disabilities to join their ranks as paid and unpaid workers, and even as management committee representatives. This extends the concept of equal opportunities beyond the more traditional barriers of race or sex discrimination. Yet for the person with a disability, this can be an isolating experience. Some charity workers without a disability become confused when asked to work alongside the people who they joined the organisation to help!! Indeed the inevitable emphasis on the tragedy of disability for fundraising purposes can be frustrating. The images of helplessness can demean the person with the disability. But things are slowly changing.

People with Disabilities: Work Opportunities and Charities

There are estimated to be over 6 million disabled people in Britain, 70% of whom develop their disability after reaching working age, and only 31% of whom are employed. Put another way, one in ten people of working age in Britain has some type of disability. Of those who are not working, some would not be able to cope with regular employment, or even occasional voluntary work. Disabled people who do want to seek work, however, even in the voluntary sector, still face prejudice or wariness about employing them.

> **"** A lot of employers assume that because you have a disability there are lots of things you can't do. They should ask disabled people what they are able to do, or how they can be enabled to do the job e.g. by getting the right equipment or the right working practices. An employee shouldn't be seen as 'disabled', but as an employee who happens to have a disability. **"**
>
> Margaret Barron Linton, Fundraising Officer, Outset

Many people still equate disability with 'handicap'. Employers often believe that disabled people are those requiring special provisions, such as wheelchair access or because they are blind. Yet 'white sticks and wheelchairs are not the norm' (Outset). Many fear that a disabled person will need more time off work due to illness. Yet experience plus research by various public and private sector employers show that in fact disabled people take less sick leave, are highly reliable and tend to be very loyal to their employers. Disability-led groups concerned with campaigning and advocacy are also addressing continuing negative perceptions. EC regulations will further require Britain to reconsider its treatment of people with disabilities.

> **"** I see disability awareness training as part of a growing tree – there are lots of different stems to the tree. It isn't just about wheelchair access, for example. It's about people having open attitudes. The barrier is not my wheelchair, but situations, access and attitudes. **"**
>
> John Kelly, worker with PHAB

If you are disabled and want to work, don't be put off by apparently negative perceptions. Attitudes are changing, new technology has altered patterns of employment, competence-led national vocational qualifications (NVQs) are making work opportunities more accessible, and underlying demographic trends, combined with the skills shortages of the 1990s, mean well trained disabled people are now being seen as an economic resource. There are also various laws, organisations and publications which now exist to help you (*see below*).

> **"** Disability isn't a reason for doing or not doing something. There'll always be difficulties, but you'll never know whether you can achieve something at the end of the day unless you give it a go. **"**
> John Kelly, worker with PHAB

But you must be sure you have employable skills to offer, since another factor limiting the employment of people with disabilities can be their lack of training and qualifications. There is no reason why virtually any one with a disability can't acquire an employable skill, whether they are, for example, completely blind or perhaps have a learning difficulty. With advances in computer and information technology many kinds of opportunities are developing, in particular for people with physical disabilities (*see section on training below*).

> **"** I suffer from juvenile rheumatoid arthritis, have five artificial joints, use a wheelchair, and am also totally blind. Most organisations will only take people for training with one disability, not two. However, St Loye's College in Exeter saw training me as a challenge! I was a guinea pig for them as they had never taken a totally blind person before. I did a commercial skills training course and all my material was transferred onto tape for me to use. The tutor had to familiarise herself with the computerised speech programme before she could start to teach me. I have passed my RSA, Pitmans and London Chamber of Commerce examinations. While training I did work experience in a bank, and after completing my course I was offered voluntary work with Exeter Health Authority. Due to St Loye's help I have now got my own flat and live independently. **"**
> Sue Stidwell, disabled volunteer worker, Devon

> **"** I have reading and spelling problems. I had difficulty finding work because of my lack of qualifications. So I did a one year course in horticulture at St Loyes College (Exeter) and got an NVQ certificate. Now I'm studying for my City & Guilds in horticulture, while doing voluntary work in a National Trust garden. If I pass I hope to find paid work in gardening, which I really enjoy, perhaps with the County Council. **"**
> Simon George, Cornwall

THE RIGHT CHARITY FOR YOU TO WORK OR VOLUNTEER IN

If you decide you would like to work in a voluntary organisation and you have a disability, you will need to take certain steps.

The key to finding the right charity for you lies in research. Each charity has its own 'culture' or style of operating and it is important that you find an organisation where you are not only committed to the cause but are comfortable with the environment and the people. Time taken considering the following may help you clarify your options:

- Which causes do you feel you could be committed to?
- Which jobs would use your current skills and experience?
- Do you need to acquire skills, or enhance or develop existing skills through training?
- Do you want to work in a charity that is concerned with disability or not?
- Do you know where and how to contact these organisations?

In the voluntary sector, currently, mainstream voluntary organisations are generally not very good employers of disabled people. Their ethos of 'charity' and 'benevolence'

> **"** I work part-time with PHAB and do voluntary work part-time. I work with young people on residential courses and also do disability training. I have a disability and I've been involved with PHAB since I was a child. **"**
> John Kelly, worker with PHAB

> **I decided to try and involve myself with local volunteer work. I went along to the local Volunteer Bureau and found them very welcoming and helpful. They directed me towards various campaigning and pressure groups, and also to the Samaritans who have accepted me as a trainee volunteer. I was also recommended to the Exeter taxi scheme for the disabled as a volunteer helper. They want a disabled person with office skills who can help to run it. The vacancy is for a co-ordinator, two to three days a week. It will be a challenge, real work, a responsibility and I'll be keeping up my skills. They will allow me to choose the equipment which I need, including a computer with speech synthesizer and a dictaphone. Next year they hope to have a paid administrator, and I'd be able to apply if I wanted to. It partly depends on the benefit situation. This year they are applying to the DSS for therapeutic earnings for me, so I won't be used as 'slave labour'. I didn't have to look for this work – they suggested me, which is really helping my confidence.**
>
> Sue Stidwell, disabled volunteer worker, Devon

> **Voluntary organisations could take a lead in employing people with disabilities to show that they can be employed successfully and that you don't necessarily need special circumstances to employ them. Then voluntary organisations could demonstrate to other employers that employing disabled people is not necessarily a problem, and that if there are any problems they can be overcome satisfactorily.**
>
> Margaret Barron Linton, Fundraising Officer, Outset

means that they may tend to see disabled people as clients, rather than as partners and active citizens. Although this situation is slowly changing, you will need to be aware of it when choosing charities to approach.

The best opportunities for disabled people to work in the voluntary sector tend to be in disability organisations, and more so in those with 'of' in their title (e.g. the **British Council of Organisations of Disabled People**, the **Greater Manchester Coalition of Disabled People**), rather than those with 'for'. Disabled people are often empowering themselves in terms of work opportunities, and in setting up voluntary organisations to fight for their needs and be advocates for them. These are the kinds of organisations which you might approach first to see about work opportunities.

Other organisations which welcome disabled people working in them, particularly as volunteers, include **Arthritis Care**, the **National Back Pain Association** (NBPA), **Self Help for People in Pain** (SHIP), and the **Disability Income Group** (DIG). However, in mid-1993 many disabled volunteers found themselves fearful of losing their invalidity benefit if they volunteered, following enquiries and letters from the **Department of Social Security** (DSS) concerning their ability to do paid work. One wheelchair user, Peggy Prior from Canterbury commented 'They (the DSS) seem to

> *We work in an environment helping people with haemophilia and with HIV/Aids arising from treatment of haemophilia. So there is understanding of people with disability and the staff are very sympathetic. It keeps my mind off my own problems, helping those with haemophilia, which is a much heavier cross to bear than having manic depression. Haemophilia starts from birth and is a lifetime condition. I didn't get manic depression until I was 17. But I'm not treated specially at all. I'm expected to pull my weight and I do. I'm treated like any other employee, but I happen to have a disability.*
>
> Tom Bradley, worker with the Haemophilia Society

be saying if disabled people do charity work they can do paid work, but it's not the same at all. With charity work, if you're not up to it, you just don't do it' (quoted in 'The Observer', 20 June 1993). The Volunteer Centre UK was seeking clarification from the DSS concerning entitlement to invalidity benefit, and other disability agencies will be involved in campaigning. If you are concerned that you might be adversely affected if you volunteer, then check with one of the disability organisations, such as the Greater London Association of Disabled People (GLAD) (see useful addresses at end).

GLAD is a London-wide forum for disability issues and works with independent, borough-based disability associations throughout London, linking through them with over 10,000 disabled Londoners. It also works with national and regional voluntary organisations on such disability issues as benefits and discrimination. GLAD is controlled by people with disabilities, and most of its staff and its management committee are disabled. Apart from providing training and consultancy to voluntary, statutory and commercial organisations, GLAD is involved in advocacy, provides an information service and publishes a newsletter: the *London Disability Guide*, and various other sources of information.

GLAD's *London Disability News* includes advertisements for jobs for disabled people. In the July/August issue for 1993 for example, **Action Disability Kensington and Chelsea**, an organisation controlled by disabled people, was seeking a new director, the post earmarked for people with disabilities only. Similarly, **Southwark Women's Aid's** advertisement for a woman disability development worker encouraged women with disabilities to apply, while pointing out that its office was 'not wheelchair accessible'. It is legal to advertise jobs for disabled people only, and employers wanting to target them can use various specialist disability publications. You should also look in the general appointments pages of national newspapers for such advertisements and see if your local authority has set up a local employment advice service for people with disabilities.

Coalitions of disabled people, run by people with disabilities, now exist in various parts of the country. Around 80 such agencies, which are members of the British Council of Organisations of Disabled People, are not only enabling people with disabilities to run their own representative organisations, but are also challenging traditional attitudes and the traditional status quo within the voluntary sector.

Apart from the possibility of working or volunteering in voluntary sector agencies in Britain, you may also find possibilities for going overseas. Organisations running work camps, for example, will consider applicants with disabilities, although acceptance will depend on the types of projects being undertaken and your particular type of disability.

LAWS RELATING TO PEOPLE WITH DISABILITIES AND EMPLOYMENT

Various employment, health and safety regulations have been introduced for disabled people. These laws were not set up to prevent the employment of people with disabilities, although they may sometimes appear to hinder someone getting a job. People may be refused employment on the outcome of a medical, for example, or because they are perceived as a fire risk! If you feel that this could be the case for you, contact your local disability rights organisation (e.g. **Committee for the Employment of People with Disabilities** – CEPD) or trades union.

The 1944 and 1958 Disabled Persons Employment Acts

The Register: the Acts set up a register of disabled people. This is voluntary and not linked to receipt of benefit etc. The main advantage of registering for employment is that you can use the services of the Employment Service.

The Quota Scheme: was introduced to assist people with disabilities to get a fair share of available jobs. It requires all employers employing over 20 people to maintain a minimum quota of 3% registered disabled people on their staff. For example, employers should not offer vacant posts to unregistered applicants if this would result in the number of registered disabled people falling below the quota.

The Approved Document M: Access and Facilities for Disabled People

This became law in June 1992. It states that non-domestic buildings (newly built or undergoing major refurbishments) must be 'reasonably' accessible for people with disabilities to gain access and to use the building.

The Companies Act 1985

This Act requires all large companies (with over 350 employees) to state in their annual report their policy on the employment and retention of people with disabilities, registered or not.

EQUAL OPPORTUNITIES

Despite continuing limitations on disabled people finding work, there is also a growing commitment to equal opportunities from within the voluntary sector. This can only be good news for you if you are a person with a disability looking for employment in the not-for-profit sector or with a charity.

Many charities have equal opportunities policies, and should be happy to have disabled volunteers and workers who will have the same requirements for support as any other person.

If you want to work with one of these charities and it clearly states that it will not discriminate on the grounds of disability, you may need to explain how it can best meet your needs. It may be of help to you, for example, to have an interpreter provided at an interview, to ask for an accessible interviewing room, or to state whatever else your particular needs may be.

You could also inform the organisation of the various services available which it can use to obtain grants to pay for any additional costs involved in enabling it to employ you. Or you could perhaps suggest contacting the local disability-led organisation which can advise on anti-discriminatory practices.

SERVICES TO ASSIST EMPLOYING PEOPLE WITH DISABILITIES

In Open Employment

The Government's Employment Service organises various services to assist employers in employing people with disabilities. It has a Code of Good Practice and produces a number of booklets containing general advice and practical suggestions. Registering as disabled is a pre-requisite to accessing these services. For application forms, contact the Disability Employment Advisor (DEA) at your local Job Centre. The DEA is a member of the Placing, Awareness and Counselling Team (or PACT) that provides an employment service for people with disabilities, and can also be found at your local Job Centre.

Your employer should also be aware of the following services:

- **Financial help with equipment or adaptations to premises:** your employer can apply for a grant of up to £6,000 to adapt premises and/or order equipment which will assist you in doing your job.
- **Loan of equipment:** you can borrow equipment from the Employment Service for the duration of your employment at no cost to yourself or your employer. For example you may need a minicom, a lap-top computer or another special aid to assist you in doing your job.
- **Fares to work:** grants are available for up to 75% of the costs of taxis or similar fares to work.
- **Reading services:** the Employment Service offers assistance with wages for a reader to assist employees with visual disabilities.

In Sheltered Employment

The Disabled Persons (Employment) Act 1944 states that provision must be made for people who are assessed as needing to work under sheltered conditions. Various schemes exist including:

- **A Job Introduction Scheme:** the Employment Service contributes to your wages for a six week trial period. Contact your local Disability Advisor.
- **Sheltered Placement Scheme:** this is where you are in open employment but where your output is lower than that of your fellow workers and you still receive a full wage. See your local Disability Employment Advisor.
- **The Shaw Trust:** this works in a similar way to the sheltered placement scheme except it is run by an independent charity.

> *" I have been doing voluntary work in a sheltered workshop since finishing my joinery training at St Loye's (Exeter) in June 1992 and getting Level 1 and 2 of the National Vocational Qualification (NVQ) in joinery. I go three days a week and get some allowances and my transport is paid for. I do joinery and cabinet making. I enjoy the work and working with my hands. I prefer using hardwood but it's very expensive. We can make things more cheaply from soft wood. I make garden chairs, cabinets, furniture and occasional tables. I hope to get paid employment. But at the moment I'm happy to keep my hands occupied, and if a job comes up, I'll be in the right place."*
>
> Robert, Dyfed

TRAINING AND RECRUITMENT ORGANISATIONS

Various agencies now exist to advise and help people with disabilities to prepare for and find work, whether in the private, public or voluntary sector. Some offer disabled people training in a range of skills, especially those involving computer technology. Some are recruitment agencies specifically for people with disabilities. The following is a selection.

> **“** Scope offers a car washing service to people living/working in the surrounding community. The customer pays the going rate for a full car valet. The people providing the service all have a learning disability and are supported by a member of staff to become increasingly independent. The project not only concentrates on developing the necessary skills for car washing, but also provides an opportunity for the workers to explore and experience features of paid employment e.g. time-keeping, quality demands, earning and banking money, etc. This is the one way that clients can evaluate their desire and readiness for open paid employment. When they wish to move on to this they register with Kensington Recruitment, a recruitment agency specialising in supported employment for people with learning disabilities. **”**
>
> Derek Orr, Scope, London

Employers' Forum on Disability

A non-profit making organisation linked to the **Prince of Wales Advisory Group on Disability**, it approaches disability from the employer's perspective. It aims to improve disabled peoples' job prospects by making it easier for employers to recruit, retain and develop people with disabilities.

Excel Employment/Excel Recruitment

A unique, equal opportunities, recruitment consultancy specialising in helping people with a disability to find paid, open employment. Excel's services are open to the entire disabled community of London, and provide counselling, help with CVs and application forms, job search and, where necessary, on-site training and job support. Excel has built up excellent relationships with many of the country's leading employers and attracts a wide range of different vacancies. The service is entirely free to applicants and is Voluntary Sector funded.

Fast-Track

A partnership between the Spastics Society, a group of major national employers, and a network of Training and Enterprise Councils (TECs) to offer 'unprecedented career opportunities' for people with disabilities. It aims to provide disabled people of graduate calibre with the skills and experience needed for managerial roles in the private, public and voluntary sectors. It offers two-year, paid, job experience through work placements, and a Diploma in Management Studies through distance learning. Participating employers include the **Wellcome Foundation** and the **Bank of England**.

Kensington Recruitment

A professional employment service and recruitment agency in London for people with learning difficulties who want to take up open, paid employment. An innovative scheme launched by the **Royal Borough of Kensington and Chelsea**, and managed by the Social Services Department, the agency supports equal opportunities and works with employers to place people with learning difficulties in paid employment. Employment workers help candidates identify their skills and job requirements, and prepare CVs, applications and for interviews. After a position is secured, on-the-job trainers support each person.

The agency has lists of suitable candidates and of employers willing to participate. The scheme is not only individualised, but also an example of close collaboration between local government and the private sector.

Mencap, Pathway Employment Service (PES)

PES provides a personalised service to people with learning disabilities. Specialised assistance is given to assess aspirations and abilities, and to put into place the level of support required to find and keep appropriate employment. Individual plans can involve preparatory training or work experience, or direct access to employment.

Employment opportunities can be obtained by people with learning disabilities by:

- being assisted in their search for work
- themselves assisting in a voluntary or paid capacity in making work viable for others
- joining mencap to run Employment Services.

Jobs which have been found for people with learning difficulties include positions in industry, retailing, horticulture, offices, service industries, catering and the voluntary sector.

Outset

Established in 1970, as a training and consultancy charity, Outset now has a network of training centres in the UK and links across Europe. It aims to provide employment and free training opportunities, by concentrating on skills involving new technology, to empower disabled people. It trains hundreds of people every year in modern office, information technology and computer skills to meet the needs of employers locally, including voluntary organisations. Over half of Outset's own staff are people with disabilities and it has a Positive Action Programme to recruit, train and promote them. It can support people with any type of disability – physical, mental, learning difficulties or HIV/Aids. It also runs customised disability awareness training courses for employers to give them 'the confidence to recruit and employ people with disabilities'.

" I have lumbar scoliosis, or curvature of the spine, am registered disabled, and have to sit in a specially designed chair, provided by PACT. I heard about this job from a former colleague who was working with Outset. It was advertised on a competitive basis, but said personal experience of disability was desirable. In fact Outset positively welcomes applications from disabled people. But for many disabled people the difficulty will be for them to get the work experience which the employer wants. Yet experience may not be as important as the skills and abilities which they have. Maybe if we had more disabled people in managerial roles, we would have more disabled people in employment."

Margaret Barron Linton, Fundraising Officer, Outset

" I get manic depression which is controlled with drugs. I was attending a day centre when I happened to pick up a leaflet by Outset about getting a job if you have a disability. I went along to Outset for an interview and they did a CV for me and then suggested me for this job at the Haemophilia Society. I went along for an interview, an Outset worker came with me, and I started the next day! It was very informal and they had been briefed about me. My disability was never talked about, which really surprised me. I haven't had any time off through illness since I began 18 months ago. I really enjoy it, it's a nice place to work, and the working conditions are therapeutic."

Tom Bradley, worker with the Haemophilia Society

St Loye's College Foundation

A registered charity, established in 1937 and based in Exeter, it trains men and women with all kinds of disabilities. This prepares them for open paid employment in all sectors, including voluntary agencies, for sheltered work, or for voluntary work, depending on individual circumstances. The Initial Training Centre offers assessment, employment rehabilitation and training, while the manufacturing unit manufactures leather goods and joinery products. The company also operates on the same campus St. Loye's School of Occupational Therapy with undergraduate and post-graduate programmes.

> *" The turning point for me was going to St Loye's. They were so supportive and the training was brilliant. I have now got my qualifications and I am living independently, with the help of carers, despite being blind and using a wheelchair. It has helped my confidence tremendously. I really feel I have to get out into the world and fight for the rights and equality that I know I am entitled to. I would say to anyone who is disabled 'get out and mix with people and show what you can do with a disability'. "*
>
> Sue Stidwell, disabled volunteer worker, Devon

St Loye's believes that to enable people with disabilities to gain employment, training for the needs, and in the skills, of the 1990s is essential. Its approach is always to stress the ability, not the disability, and to provide training best suited to each person's needs and potential. Operating like a work place, residential training programmes include catering, commercial skills, electronics, engineering, horology, horticulture, information technology, joinery and store keeping.

Scope

A day service for adults with learning disabilities based in North Kensington, London, using local resources such as adult education colleges, libraries, sports centres, etc. as well as its own base. It aims to support 58 people in developing skills for daily living and leisure.

Workable

A consortium of voluntary sector providers whose overall aim is to improve employment opportunities for people with disabilities through the exchange of ideas and information, and by working together to develop and publicise good practice and minimum standards in the field.

> *I graduated from the University of Lancaster in 1983 and worked in Yorkshire for some years before moving to London. I was employed firstly with the RNIB [Royal National Institute for the Blind] and then in the private sector as a Placement and Marketing Officer with the London Chamber of Commerce and Industry. After being made redundant in November 1991, I worked in two part-time jobs but found my career was not going anywhere.*
>
> *Consequently I decided to study full-time at the University of East London for the Post Graduate Diploma in Careers Guidance. Through my two careers office placements I developed an interest in vocational guidance with people with special needs. I also made many friends! I completed my diploma in July 1993, having already applied for five jobs and received interviews for two. I am happy to say that I chose Workable where I now work as the Co-ordinator to the Graduate Support Scheme.*

Disabled worker, Workable

USEFUL ADDRESSES

The following agencies may be of use to you:

Employers' Forum on Disability, 5 Cleveland Place, London SW1Y 6JJ, tel: 071-321 6591

Excel Employment/Recruitment, 2 High Street, Hornsey, London N8 7PD, tel: 081-348 8141

Fast-Track, 16 Fitzroy Square, London W1P 4HQ, tel: 071-387 9571

Outset, Drake house, 18 Creekside, London SE8 3DZ, tel: 081-692 7141

The Royal Association for Disability and Rehabilitation, 25 Mortimer Street, London W1N 8AB, tel: 071-637 5400

St Loye's College Foundation, Topsham Road, Exeter EX2 6EP, tel: 0392-55428

Scope, 1-9 St Marks Road, London W11 1RG, tel: 071-727 4765

Workable, Room C05, Victoria House, 98 Victoria Street, London SW1E 5JL, tel: 071-915 0054

All the addresses below are organisations run by people with disabilities who have full-time staff. The information officers will be able to advise you of the best local contact for you to start your enquiries.

Asian People with Disabilities Alliance, Ground Floor, Willesden Hospital, Harlesdon Road, London NW10 3RY, tel: 081-459 5793.

Avon Coalition of Disabled People, c/o Easton Community Centre, Kilburn Street, Easton, Bristol BS5 6AW, tel: 0272-412063.

Birmingham Disability Resource Centre, Bierton Road Centre, Bierton Road, South Yardley, Birmingham B25 8PQ, tel: 021-789 7365, minicom: 021-789 9230.

The British Council of Organisations of Disabled People, De Bradelei House, Chapel Street, Belper, Derbyshire DE5 1AR, tel: 0773-828182, minicom: 0773-828195.

British Deaf Association, 38 Victoria Place, Carlisle, Cumbria CA1 1HU, tel: 0228-48844 (voice/minicom).

Derbyshire Centre for Integrated Living, Long Close, Cemetery Lane, Ripley, Derbyshire DE5 3HY, tel: 0773-740246.

Greater London Association of Disabled People (GLAD), 336 Brixton Road, London SW9 7AA, tel: 071-274 0107.

Greater Manchester Coalition of Disabled People, Unit 33, Cariocca Enterprises Ltd, 2 Hellidon Close, Ardwick, Manchester M12 4AH, tel: 061-273 5154/5.

The Lothian Centre for Integrated Living, 13 Johnston Terrace, Edinburgh EH1 2PW, tel: 031-225 3555.

PUBLICATIONS

There are very few national publications available, but London-based publications do have useful information for people living elsewhere in Britain. Many of the large, national voluntary organisations have their own newsletters etc. dealing with a specific area of disability and you could contact those which are relevant. You could also try public libraries in your own area to see if they can suggest anything specific to your part of the country.

Directory of London Disability Organisations

Directory of Volunteer and Employment Opportunities, by Jan Brownfoot and Frances Wilks, published by the Directory of Social Change, includes organisations concerned with disability

Disability Now, published by the Spastics Society, contains job advertisements

The Employment Service (Department of Employment), has various booklets, information on PACT schemes, etc.

London Disability Guide, contains lists of organisations and publications

London Disability News

Third Sector, the news magazine for people in the charity world, published by Art Publishing International, includes articles for people with disabilities.

12
ADVICE GIVING, COUNSELLING & WORKING ON A TELEPHONE HELPLINE

The last few years have seen an enormous increase in the number of voluntary agencies who offer advice, information and counselling. Some of this is face-to-face, some via telephone helplines. Some use paid staff to give the advice, but many involve volunteers. Advice giving, whether by telephone or face-to-face, offers an attractive opportunity for those who want to do something useful and who enjoy dealing with people and helping to solve problems.

> *You basically need to be prepared to listen to someone and not to judge them in any way. The rewards are that you get such a lot of trust and you meet all sorts of people – from all walks of life. I've loved doing it and it's had a tremendous impact on my life in terms of direction and a change of career.*
>
> Sarah, Volunteer with Victim Support

It is important to understand the difference between advice giving and counselling before you look for an opportunity to get involved so that you know exactly what you are looking for.

GIVING ADVICE AND INFORMATION

Many problems in life can be solved by getting the appropriate information at the right time. This can include advice on a variety of subjects (e.g., debt, consumer affairs, housing and homelessness, social security benefits, access to justice).

The emphasis is on practical information rather than counselling. Advice can suggest:

- what courses of action are open
- what sources of further help are available
- what to do and where to go next.

Many organisations offer this sort of advice. The largest is the **Citizens Advice Bureau** which employs 20,000 volunteers. Most of these work as advisors and receive extensive training.

❝ *The Portobello Project gives practical advice on a whole range of issues specifically to do with young people. Often they ask us:*
- *how do I get benefit?*
- *how do I apply for a job?*
- *where can I find careers advice?*
- *how can I find somewhere to live?*

We can't give in-depth counselling but we can offer signposting for information we don't have to hand. ❞
Gill Fitzhugh, volunteer, the Portobello Project

Personal Qualities and Training

To be an effective advice giver you need to have a friendly, open approach and to enjoy talking to people.

If you have practical knowledge of a subject such as housing or disability, this is always useful. However, most organisations offer training. This is essential because problems can be complex and the response can involve access to highly technical information (such as housing and welfare benefits rules). Sometimes solutions require asking questions in a sympathetic way to get to the root of the problem.

How to Volunteer?

To volunteer, contact either:

- your local Volunteer Bureau
- your local Citizens Advice Bureau (CAB)

Both these numbers should be in the local telephone directory or available from the local library.

Alternatively, if you know of a charity whose cause you particularly support, you may wish to contact them direct. **The Federation of Independent Advice Centres** (FIAC), Concourse House, Lime Street, Liverpool L1 1NT, tel: 051-709 7444, acts as a referral network of mostly small, local, independent, advice-giving agencies.

> **"** I became manager of my local CAB (Citizens Advice Bureau) in 1985. My staff consisted of fourteen advice workers and four administrative workers – all volunteers. I had to ensure that there was adequate supervision and support for the workers, and that there was the provision of a competent and sympathetic advice service to the local community. In 1992 the four CABs around the Barnet area dealt with 64,000 enquiries – Social Security, Consumer and Debt being the largest categories. Money advice and debt problems seemed to overwhelm us at times and the demand for help from the CABs has never been greater. **"**
>
> Joan Price, CAB (Citizens Advice Bureau) volunteer

COUNSELLING – IN FACE-TO-FACE SITUATIONS

Some of the problems people face include emotional or psychological distress. In-depth counselling can help people (usually called clients) to see their particular situation in a new light and to face the future with renewed hope. Generally, a client will be seen by the same counsellor for a number of sessions face-to-face. It will probably involve:

- getting to know the client
- exploring the client's feelings and needs
- building a relationship of trust and acceptance.

Counselling is not about offering solutions or giving personal advice.

There is a wide range of agencies that offer counselling for problems such as AIDS, alcohol, drugs, bereavement, suicide, family and relationship problems, to name but a few.

What is the difference between Counselling and Psychotherapy? Counselling and Psychotherapy overlap to some extent. The objective of Psychotherapy is to tackle problems at deeper psychological levels. It is usually practised by qualified professionals who have undergone years of training. Quite a few volunteers do go on to become professional counsellors or psychotherapists. Working in a counselling capacity for a voluntary agency is seen as a good way of gaining experience for such a career.

> **"** My years as a bereavement counsellor were an important bridge from my previous job as a nurse to becoming a psychotherapist. The training that was offered was of high quality and it gave me an insight into what doing this job full-time would be like. **"**
> Anne, trainee psychotherapist at Regent's College, London.

Voluntary counselling agencies play a role of vital importance to the nation's mental health because they are able to offer free or low cost counselling to people who would not otherwise be able to afford the cost of psychotherapy.

How often do you see your Client?

Styles of counselling within voluntary agencies vary – some see their clients once a week for a limited number of sessions, usually between six and twelve. Others may be able to offer help on a longer term basis. Some offer help in times of crisis. Some agencies make a charge to the client according to income, some ask for a donation and others are free.

What Personal Qualities do I need and what Training and Support will I receive?

To be an effective counsellor, you will need to have the following qualities:

- an ability to listen
- an open-minded outlook
- a capacity to be non-judgemental
- an empathy with other people and their problems.

In addition you will also need a willingness to examine yourself and your motivations. You need to be sure that you yourself have worked through a personal crisis or problem before you can counsel others about it. As in all voluntary work, reliability and commitment are very important.

> *"You must go into counselling with an open mind. You must also be prepared to be exhausted by the work and to be very humbled by the experiences you learn that children have."*
> Karen, Volunteer Counsellor, ChildLine

Training and Selection

Most voluntary agencies which recruit volunteers for counselling spend a great deal of time in selecting and training the right people. Typically you will be invited to a Selection Day. Information about the organisation will be given and there will be one-to-one interviews as well as group discussions. You will probably also have to fill in an application form and may have to have a police check as well.

Training usually takes place over a period of weeks or months. The object of training is to enable you to do your job as a counsellor as effectively as possible. Generally it will include:

- the policy of the organisation, its commitments and ideals
- the development of listening skills
- role-playing of various sorts of client problems
- understanding the importance of confidentiality
- the encouragement of self-knowledge and understanding.

> *"The training is an eight week course of about three hours a week. The course acts as a vetting procedure and gives both sides time to decide if they are right for each other. You also have a police check on your background. You are tested in one-to-one situations with role-plays and in groups. You get feed-back and comments on your skills and those areas you might have problems with. Some people do drop out of the course."*
> Malcolm, volunteer counsellor, ChildLine

Support and Supervision

Most voluntary organisations offer their counsellors both support and supervision. It can be very harrowing working with a person who is going through an acutely difficult time and the counsellor needs to have someone who is experienced to turn to. You should check whether this kind of support is offered before taking up any volunteer post.

How do I go about choosing the Right Organisation to work for?

Each organisation will have its own set of objectives and beliefs. It is worth acquainting yourself fully with these before applying. Questions to ask yourself could include:

- What are the organisation's principles and approach to the problem and do I agree with them?
- What is the time commitment and can I realistically meet this?
- Do I possess sufficient personal maturity to be able to undertake this sort of work?
- Are training and on-going support provided?
- Does the organisation pay expenses and/or a salary of some sort?
- Is there any possibility of developing a volunteer job into a paid position?

❝ *You have to be prepared to commit yourself because it could be quite some time before you see any paid work come out of it, if that's what you want.* **❞**
Sid, volunteer counsellor, ChildLine

Sources of help

Your local volunteer bureau may be able to direct you to organisations in your area needing volunteers.

"The Directory of Volunteer and Employment Opportunities" (available from the Directory of Social Change) has a section on Caring/Counselling which lists many organisations that involve volunteer counsellors.

BEING A COUNSELLOR – JENNY RINDELL'S STORY

"I've been a volunteer counsellor with Relate, an agency which offers counselling in relationships, for three and a half years now. It came out of my work as a Further Education lecturer. I did a lot of work with women returners and I saw how their life changes were affecting their relationships. When women go back to work, often their horizons open up whereas their husbands, may be closing down, possibly facing redundancy. Relationships can fall apart.

I did an RSA course in counselling skills for people using counselling in their work. Then I did two and half years training with Relate – it's a modular course, you fit it round your life. Training involves skills practice and personal development work. When you start counselling there's a lot of supervision and support. You never really stop having supervision.

Most counselling training you have to pay for yourself. The good thing about working with Relate is that you train for free in exchange for a voluntary commitment. You get to meet a cross-section of society and a variety of multi-cultural groups. Clients who come for counselling pay a voluntary contribution – they pay what they can afford and nobody is turned away.

The work is so interesting. It's given me a transferable training and a personal understanding. It has also given me a career structure, because I am going to become a part-time supervisor in a couple of months time. This is in addition to my voluntary commitment to the agency of three hours a week.

I brought my own life experience, a desire to work with people and an understanding of myself. My teaching background gave me an insight into how people learn and change. Working with people with low self-esteem, which is the case with many women returners, was very valuable experience because most of the people who come for counselling have low self-esteem.

Relate as an agency has really taken on board the need for people to work voluntarily. It's structured so that you can work full-time as well as volunteer. Many more men are coming into the agency as volunteer counsellors which can only be good. The most important thing for any counsellor to realise is that you are also a client in another context. In other words, you never stop learning about yourself and the way you work."

The **British Association of Counselling** (BAC), 1 Regent Place, Rugby, Warwickshire CV21 2PJ, tel: 0788-578328, sets standards for counselling nationally in practice and training.

Working on a Telephone Helpline

Every year, over five million calls are made to telephone helplines. Some offer support, others information and advice, but all use the telephone as their primary source of contact. Working on a telephone helpline is often rewarding and stimulating, but can also be frustrating and challenging.

There are three main types of helpline though many fall into more than one category. Most run on a voluntary basis, but some offer payment either for expenses or as a salary.

1. Self-Help Helplines

These lines are run by and operate for those affected by a particular set of circumstances. They are often set up for sufferers of a particular illness or family difficulty. Examples include **Parents Anonymous, Release, Acceptance**. They provide support by sharing experiences and offering advice, information and on-going support.

To help on this type of line you normally need to have an association with the cause, either as a sufferer, or a user, or as a relative. Most of these lines are run on a voluntary basis. Many will offer training to volunteers.

> **"** I wanted to talk through problems with someone else who had faced them and come to terms with them. **"**

2. Information and Advice Lines

These lines are for people who need information and advice about a subject or who need support and advice about the best paths to follow. An example of this is **DIAL**, the Disabled Information and Advice lines run by local DIAL groups.

On occasion such information/advice lines will provide practical support on the caller's behalf, but most offer further information and signposting rather than doing anything practical for the caller. Some of these lines employ full-time counsellors, who need to have formal qualifications in counselling. Others will train you.

> **"** I wanted information about where to go and advice on what possibilities existed for me. **"**

3. Caring Stranger Lines

These lines offer independent and anonymous confidential support on a range of problems. They tend to offer time, space and a chance to talk without giving advice. Examples of these include the **Samaritans** and **ChildLine**.

Most of these lines are run by volunteers with the back-up of paid staff. One of the primary qualifications is the ability to be a good listener. Training is always given.

> **"** I wanted to talk to someone who had the time to listen without giving me advice or telling me their life story. **"**

What do I need to work on a Telephone Helpline?

Before applying to work on a telephone helpline, you might like to ask yourself the following questions:

- have I got time to spare? Most helplines ask for a regular and on-going commitment

- can I respect other people's confidentiality?

- can I cope with the calls? If you've recently been through a crisis, allow yourself time to come to terms with it. Later on, your experience may be very valuable

- can you cope with other people's problems? For instance, if someone is threatening suicide, could you live with not knowing the outcome?

- do I have sufficient maturity? Most helplines have no age restrictions, but it is unlikely you will be accepted if you are very young

- what am I like as a person? Working on a helpline involves tolerance, open-mindedness and acceptance of others

- am I a good listener? Since you are talking to people on the telephone, the ability to listen is vitally important.

- why do I want to do it? It is important to be aware of your motivation.

> **❝** On a shift you take maybe six or seven calls and the length of them varies greatly. You also spend a lot of time writing up. Some children who are extremely disturbed and call regularly are allocated special counsellors. You have to take a very broad range of calls and problems. You have to expect anything and not be surprised. You can hear some very painful stuff. There are lots of sexual abuse calls and physical abuse, too. One of the biggest problems is bullying in schools.**❞**
>
> Sid, volunteer counsellor, ChildLine

What Training and Support will I receive?

No organisation operating a helpline should put you straight on to the phones. Training is essential, and covers a wide variety of possible situations depending on the type of helpline.

Training is usually free and takes place in small groups over a number of weeks or months. Aspects covered normally include:

- the policy and ideals of the organisation
- the development of listening skills
- skills practice in acting out possible situations
- when to give information and how to find it
- how to cope with 'emotional pressures' after a call
- the importance of confidentiality.

Most people find the training process itself very challenging but ultimately personally very rewarding. In addition to training, you will probably start on a helpline with an experienced 'operator' who will support you through those first nerve-racking shifts.

Support for all those answering a helpline is crucial. Without it, you run the risk of taking on unbearable emotional pressures. All helplines should (and most do) have an excellent network of support. For example, there will probably be opportunities for de-briefing with a supervisor after a shift.

In addition, as issues, needs and technology all change, continuing training is needed to update you and keep your approach relevant. The helpline will normally provide this: it could range from inviting outside speakers to full-blown refresher courses. Some people go on to take longer counselling courses providing qualifications so that they can move to a paid career in counselling, including face-to-face work with clients.

> **❝** There is always half an hour at the end of a shift so we can talk about things and go home as empty of ChildLine as possible. The supervisors are very good at giving support. **❞**
> *Malcolm, volunteer counsellor, ChildLine*

> **❝** I wanted to contribute something back. Childhood is a very vulnerable time. I'm still learning a lot about my own childhood and myself. I'm also developing my skills as a counsellor. It gives me a feeling of purpose compared to the lethargy I felt when I took voluntary redundancy. **❞**
> *Malcolm, volunteer counsellor, ChildLine*

Where do I go from here?

If you decide that working on a telephone helpline is what you would really like to do, you will need to research the options. Ask yourself:

- What sort of telephone helpline would I like to work for? Can I work within their principles and practices?
- What agencies operate in my area?
- Do they pay expenses and/or a salary or are they purely voluntary?
- Do they offer training, support and on-going training?

SOURCES OF INFORMATION

Your local volunteer bureau (address in local telephone directory) may be able to direct you to organisations in your area needing volunteers.

The **Volunteer Centre UK**, 29 Lower Road, Berkhamsted, Hertfordshire HP24 2AB (tel. 0442-87311) can undertake searches of local organisations for individuals.

Alternatively, you may wish to approach some of the larger organisations directly, e.g. **ChildLine, Victim Support, The Samaritans**.

Both the *"Directory of Volunteer and Employment Opportunities"* and the *"Voluntary Agencies Directory"* list organisations which are involved with telephone counselling. Both are available from the Directory of Social Change.

BOOKS FOR FURTHER READING

The Gentle Art of Listening, Counselling Skills for Volunteers by Janet K. Ford and Phillippa Merriman (Bedford Square Press)

Room to Talk, Room to Listen – a Beginner's Guide to Analysis. Therapy and Counselling by Tony Lake and Fran Acheson (Bedford Square Press)

Person-Centred Counselling in Action by Dave Means and Brian Thorne (Sage Publications, Counselling in Action series).

13
STARTING YOUR OWN ORGANISATION

The traditional routes for those seeking employment in the voluntary sector are to look for and get a paid job, or to find work as a volunteer that develops skills which may eventually lead on to a paid job.

There is another option, which is for you yourself to create your own employment opportunities in the voluntary sector. This can be done in two ways:

- starting your own voluntary organisation
- providing a service which will be used by voluntary organisations.

At a time of high unemployment, when it may be difficult to find a job through traditional routes, the option of setting up on your own is certainly worth considering. It may be that you personally will not reap the rewards of your effort in financial terms but you will hopefully create employment for others and considerable experience for yourself.

WHY START A VOLUNTARY ORGANISATION?

The starting off point for setting up your own organisation should not be the desire to create employment for yourself. The motivating factor should be a concern with a particular problem and an enthusiasm to do something about it. Your enthusiasm will be a key point in getting other people to give their time and resources, so only go ahead if you can give

100% of your enthusiasm to the cause. As well as this commitment, you will also need:

- to be an effective organiser
- to have the ability to motivate people
- to be able to obtain resources.

Later on, you may find that as founder of the organisation, you have created the opportunity for yourself to be appointed by the trustees as its first co-ordinator or director. If you end up being paid to do the work, the decision to appoint you and the terms on which you will be remunerated will be decided not by your desire for employment or remuneration, but by the trustees or managing committee of the organisation. It is their responsibility to take such a decision.

Setting Up

The key to the first stage is research. First of all you will need to:

- identify and define the needs or problems that your organisation will address
- see what others are doing about the problem or issue – be very sure that you are not going to duplicate some other charity's work
- look at what provision there is in your own area.

When you have done your research, and decided you still want to go ahead, you will need the following:

- a group of people – who share your concerns and aspirations, who are prepared to act as a working group and eventually become the founding committee
- some sort of constitution – which sets out your aims and objectives and the methods by which the organisation will operate
- a legal structure – for the organisation. You might decide to be an Association or a Society. You might set yourself up as a Trust with a trust deed. You might incorporate as a Company limited by guarantee or an Industrial and Provident Society – both these formats are suitable for larger organisations. You may need to take advice on writing the constitution. You might get hold of a model constitution or

adapt a constitution of a similar organisation to your own requirements. This is often the best starting point
- open a bank account – so that you can deposit any money you collect. The bank will require sight of your constitution first, before giving you account facilities.

The next step is to:
- get started on the work
- raise the money you need, either from contributions amongst yourselves, or through subscriptions, donation and grants.

THE PORTOBELLO TRUST

"I taught in a city school for years and did individual tutoring for sixth formers. I found that deep seated problems were thrown up which needed more than just the school to tackle. Looking around I found quite a few voluntary agencies who did various forms of youth work. Most of them had glossy brochures but not a lot of substance. Finally I hit upon the Portobello Project which was a bit scruffy but was doing splendid work.

Out of the work with the Project I realised that unemployed city kids needed more help and the Portobello Trust was formed in 1986 with a local priest, a businessman, an accountant and someone from the Kensington and Chelsea Chamber of Commerce. The Trust works with young people helping them with problems such as high unemployment, inadequate education, discrimination and an unstable home life.

When our revenue funding was reduced and the Council didn't take over, we had to go to the Community. We got massive community involvement – around 500 people, including local businesses, are supporters and do various things such as giving advice, gifts in kind, gifts in time or gifts in money.

The Portobello Trust works closely with other agencies such as the Portobello Project and Portobello Houseshare providing services such as business and employment training, life skills training and housing for disadvantaged young people. Since 1986 at least 450 small businesses have been created and are still going. The local economy has greatly benefited too. We are one of the most vital local charities around. The good thing about voluntary organisations is that they are not trapped by bureaucracy, they can move with flexibility and speed and change things very quickly."

Gill Fitzhugh, the Portobello Trust.

In the UK, we have complete freedom to associate, provided that the purposes of the association are within the law. It is individuals coming together in this way which have created such national charities as **Oxfam**, **The Spastics Society** and **The National Trust**. Every year, some 4,000, new charitable bodies are formed. There are also many new groups which do not become charities. Some do not survive very long or operate at only a low level. The success of the organisation will depend on the following factors:

- the enthusiasm and commitment of the founding group – as well as their skills
- the success in meeting the need, and the recognition of this by others
- the ability to attract members, supporters or donors.

Becoming a Charity

Not all voluntary organisations are charities. But, having decided to set up your own organisation, you may wish to have charitable status. This will bring a range of benefits, including:

- the ability to receive donations from individuals and companies tax effectively through covenants and Gift Aid
- an 80% reduction in the rates payable on any property occupied by the organisation for its work
- access to charitable funds and grants when the grant-making body only gives its support to charities
- the ability to say that you are a charity when soliciting funds – this can add credibility to your appeal.

To be a charity, a number of conditions must be met:

- the objects, or purposes of your organisation must be charitable in law. You may need professional help in deciding these and drawing up your constitution
- the organisation must exist for public benefit
- the main purpose of the organisation should not be to campaign, and the organisation should not engage in 'political activity'.
- the trustees or managing committee of the organisation should receive no remuneration for their work as trustees. The constitution will normally have a clause prohibiting this.

For those seeking charitable registration, the **Charity Commission** has a range of explanatory literature.

BLISS – BABY LIFE SUPPORT SYSTEMS

"After I graduated, I had a career in Personnel Management (Public and commercial sector) and taught in a school for special needs. After two years teaching I became a mother and the birth was dangerous. A few months later, by an extraordinary chance, I saw an article about the lack of facilities for babies in special care. I felt I'd been lucky that my child was all right. I wrote to ask if I could help.

I found that 70 other people had also written, and I wrote to all of them inviting them to a meeting. Twenty people turned up and twelve of them became committee members. We had a solicitor, a bookkeeper, someone interested in medicine and someone who was interested in producing a newsletter. At that meeting we decided to launch as a charity, supplying equipment for babies in special care and training. We found a name for ourselves – BLISS, which stands for Baby Life Support Systems and were registered as a charity in three months.

The personal qualities you need are enthusiasm, commitment and the ability to work creatively with others. The team is always the thing that counts. You're starting something new, it's exciting but it's a step in the dark.

To begin with we raised small sums of money. An international Food Evening brought in £125 (this was 1979!) and a Bring and Buy Sale £50. Our income climbed steadily. The first year it was £12,000 and the second £75,000. 75% of support came from publicity and we had 50 fundraising groups. We all pulled together – we all had special jobs and all of us were home based. By the time I left in 1991, the annual income was three quarters of a million. As I'd been at the helm for over a decade it is was right that I left then because the charity needed to develop in a different way.

If you set about things in a positive way, you can make a difference in life and you can make something happen that wouldn't have otherwise. If you start a charity, you are at the bottom, and you can only go up. You need a vision... a grassroots swell began BLISS. We were focused, voluntary but not amateur."

Susanna Cheal, Executive Vice-President of BLISS

Running the Organisation

Once the organisation has been constituted, the rules for running it will be set out in the constitution. In particular, you should note:

- how trustees or managing committee members are to be appointed, and any special roles (such as Chair, Treasurer, or Secretary)
- membership (if you have it), and the rights conferred on members
- requirements and procedures for holding annual and extraordinary general meetings
- preparation and auditing of the accounts.

Most organisations exist on the efforts put in by the committee and by volunteers. If you have the resources available, you can offer to reimburse the reasonable out-of-pocket expenses incurred by committee members and volunteers. There may come a time when the work of the organisation gets so substantial that you find you may need:

- to employ staff to do the work
- to pay someone with the appropriate professional or technical expertise
- to appoint a director.

The appointment of a director is a matter for the committee to decide. As a founder of the organisation you may well be a committee member too. If you are to be appointed as the director, you can play no part in making any decision on your employment (as there would be a conflict of interest). If you become a paid employee of a charity, you will have to resign as a committee member.

Start up Funding

At the start you may find you need very little money and you can rely on the efforts put in by you and your colleagues. You may find that the small amounts of money that you do need can be collected from amongst yourselves. If you need to raise more than this, there are two possibilities:

- seeking a local grant such as a local trust or community chest fund

---

In 1992, 4,681 new charities were started. Some will go on to employ staff and may even become household names in the future.

- attracting supporters and/or local businesses to your cause and asking them to contribute.

One of your aims at this stage should be to look at future funding requirements so that you can start to develop a strategy for fundraising. A business plan, forecasting your cash flow and showing your incomings and outgoings, is a useful tool for doing this. You may need specialist help to prepare this. Help is often available through banks or Business Enterprise Schemes.

If the main work of the organisation is to raise funds, you may feel that you should be paid some form of remuneration based on your success as a fundraiser. This is a difficult situation for two reasons:

- The Charity Commissioners are unhappy about 'commission fundraising' where the fundraiser is paid a percentage of what is raised. They feel that this misleads the donors who believe that all the money they give is going to the cause.
- Under the 1992 Charities Act, if you are being paid but not as an employee of the organisation, you will be deemed a professional fundraiser. The terms of the arrangement between you and the organisation must be indicated to donors when money is being solicited.

Providing Services to a Voluntary Organisation

There is a trend nowadays towards contracting work out on a freelance or project basis. This is because many companies do not want to take on the long-term responsibility of hiring staff. The voluntary sector is no exception and charity recruitment specialists have noticed that many charities are now seeking to recruit people on a fixed term basis to carry out a specific task.

You may have a particular skill or expertise which you can offer to voluntary organisations on a freelance or consultancy basis. Skills might include:

- fundraising
- PR
- marketing and selling
- research
- print and design
- editing
- human resources
- training.

LONDON PRISON CREATIVE AND COUNSELLING TRUST

"I had an idea, an embryonic vision of providing therapy for prisoners and ex-offenders. In my voluntary work as Assistant Chaplain at Wandsworth Prison, it struck me that many people who ended up in the prison system had been in care or had been abused. It seemed to me important to offer them some hope for the future. Last summer I set up the London Prison Creative and Counselling Trust which offers counselling, drama, music and art therapy to ex-offenders and prisoners.

I am a person who is able to open a lot of doors by energy and without a lot of knowledge. My background is in advertising – I knew about product marketing and researching a new product. I've also worked in television where my task was to research and sell programme ideas. Both these skills are very useful in my work with the Trust.

I had learnt how to write a business plan when I was in advertising. I also got a good simple leaflet together – easy to read and with, I hope, a clear sense of purpose. I deliberately didn't put too much information into it – I wanted it to be a teaser, something that would provoke people into contacting the Trust to find out more.

The Trust is a fairly radical idea. I needed to challenge perceptions and yet market the idea in a way that wouldn't put people off. There is also a Christian basis, which is written into the constitution, and this needed to be put across sensitively.

Whenever you start a new venture, it is important to identify your own skills and apply them as well as realising those areas where you are not so strong. The art then is to involve people who have what you lack. I chose my trustees on this basis. There is a lawyer, a well-established businessman, a counsellor, an art lecturer and a woman who is both a volunteer for another charity and a personal friend. When I had read the Charity Commissioners' booklet on *Starting a Charity* I got in touch with a lawyer who helped me with filling out the forms. We decided to become a limited liability company as well as a charity.

One of the things you go through when you set something up is the feeling that it's pointless. There are set-backs. At 4 am things can seem very bleak and lonely. At the moment I am working in a voluntary capacity, although we have had several grants, and I hope to be able to become a paid employee soon. I am also looking at a trading activity which will be called Light for Life to help fund us through the next three years."

Liza Davies, founder of the London Prison Creative and Counselling Trust.

Making the transition to contract work can be difficult for some people as there is an element of uncertainty about it. The rewards, however, are potentially very great:

- you will probably be able to negotiate a slightly higher rate of pay than you would receive as an employee (to compensate for pension, NI contributions etc.)
- you will gain a variety of experience in several different organisations
- it may well lead on to a full-time job if resources become available.

In order to set about marketing yourself, you will need:

- a brochure of some sort, which sets out what you can offer
- a financial plan, so that you know how much you should charge
- samples of your work and endorsements
- active marketing, networking and persistence.

You may find that you can get some form of Enterprise Allowance or grant for development of a new business. If you require business planning advice, contact your nearest **Enterprise Agency** (address from **Business in the Community**, 8 Stratton Street, London W1X 5FD).

FURTHER INFORMATION

Advice on constitutions can be obtained from the Legal Department of the **National Council for Voluntary Organisations**, 8 All Saints Street, London N1 9RL.

Information on charity status can be obtained from the **Charity Commission**, 57-60 Haymarket, London SW1Y 4QX.

If you are putting in time as a volunteer, and if you are unemployed and in receipt of benefit, you may continue to claim benefit and to receive some small remuneration in addition. There have been recent changes in the rules concerning benefit, so contact your local Volunteer Bureau or Department of Social Security office for further information.

FURTHER READING

Charity Status: a practical handbook, £7.95

Starting and Running a Voluntary Organisation, £3.95

Voluntary but not Amateur, £7.95

Just About Managing, £10.95

The Effective Trustee: roles and responsibilities, £7.95

All available from the **Directory of Social Change**, Radius Works, Back Lane, London NW3 1HL.

14
BECOMING A TRUSTEE

Serving as a member of the Management Committee or as a Trustee is one form of volunteering. Trustees are the people who ultimately control the organisation, even though they may employ staff or use volunteers to carry out the actual work. Trustees are almost always unpaid.

How trustees are appointed and how long they serve depends on the constitution of the organisation. In some organisations the trustees are elected by the membership and serve for a limited term. In others they are appointed by the existing trustees with no time limit. Some of the trustees may be appointed as representatives of other organisations or funding bodies.

" In the 1980s the Portobello Project in Notting Hill (West London) had been doing lots of work with unemployed young people who had no hope of getting jobs. It found them work in the local community and helped some of them set up as self-employed businesses. Then its funding from ILEA was cut so it had to cut its staff. I was chair of the Management Group and in August 1986 we set up the Portobello Trust and raised money to pay the staff. We now have 12 trustees. For me it's almost a full-time job and commitment. I got involved because of my belief that when we think of inner cities we should not think of areas of violence, dereliction, unemployment and depression, but as they could be: places of excitement, challenge and creativity."

Gill Fitzhugh, The Portobello Trust.

Some charities are looking for suitable people to serve as trustees, whether to replace retiring trustees or because they are finding it difficult to attract people with sufficient commitment, time or relevant qualifications. If you feel strongly about a cause, have some appropriate experience and can bring an important skill to the organisation (such as financial or legal skills, marketing, fundraising, property management, etc.), then they may be happy to consider you as a trustee.

If you find that no organisation exists for the particular cause in which you are interested, you could set up a trust yourself.

If you do want to serve as a trustee, you need to understand the legal responsibilities of the role and the amount of time and commitment that it will involve.

> **“** To become a trustee you **must** be aware of the implications. It is terribly important to look at the other trustees and the group. I would not get involved with a group of trustees who didn't share the same aims and values. There must be a shared perception and vision. **”**
> Gill Fitzhugh, The Portobello Trust

If you still feel this is the right step, then approach the organisation of your choice direct and ask. Being a trustee is a rewarding role in itself. Together with your co-trustees you are at the helm of the organisation and in a position actually to do something about a problem or need. Apart from what you contribute you are also likely to learn a lot, whatever your background. It can also be a help if you are looking for employment in the voluntary sector, as it adds to your experience and demonstrates your commitment.

> **“** I have been with Action Aid 13 years as a trustee. It has taught me a great deal. I've learnt about the differences and complexities of managing a voluntary organisation compared with a commercial company, including the different cultures. I've had to develop an understanding of Charity and Trustee law, and also about managing people who are motivated by many factors, but not necessarily money. I have also brought things to my own job that I have learnt from being a trustee. **”**
> Rodney Buse, Trustee and Chairman of Action Aid and Group Personnel Director, W H Smith

The Role of Trustees

The trustees of an organisation undertake four quite separate roles:

- the **Trustee Role** – responsibility for seeing that the organisation operates properly within its constitution, acts at all times in the interests of its beneficiaries and applies its funds for the purposes of the organisation and for which they were raised.
- the **Management Role** – involves supervising the financial affairs and performance, through normal accounting, reporting, monitoring and evaluation procedures.
- the **Strategic Role** – trustees give the organisation direction and set policies and priorities to meet needs effectively within available resources.
- the **Volunteer Role** – trustees act in a voluntary capacity to support and help the organisation's work. When resources are stretched, their contribution can be crucial: many organisations operate largely through their trustees' efforts.

What Trustees are Expected to Do

Management committee members are expected to perform two main groups of tasks: tasks to fulfil **legal duties** and **managerial tasks**.

Tasks to fulfil Legal Duties

- to ensure that the organisation pursues its objectives as set out in its governing instrument
- to have read and understood the governing instrument (constitution)
- to act at all times in the interests of the beneficiaries
- to understand the legal responsibilities of the committee member
- to make sure that the organisation acts within the law: as an employer, in respect of equal opportunities, in meeting health and safety requirements, as a charity and so on
- to ensure that all money and assets are prudently managed and used in pursuit of the objects of the organisation

The trustees of a charity or the management committee of a voluntary organisation are ultimately responsible for *everything* that the organisation does.

- to make sure that money is spent for the purposes for which it was given
- to ensure that the organisation accounts for its activities to its funders, the Charity Commissioners, its members, the local community and others as required
- to work jointly with the other committee members
- to ensure that the organisation manages its affairs reasonably and properly
- to work in the interests of the organisation and not for personal gain
- to ensure that the committee takes proper professional advice on matters in which it does not have competence.

Managerial Tasks

Vision and direction

- to understand and be committed to the organisation's mission, ensuring that it pursues this

Financial duties

- to read and understand the financial information about the organisation and to ensure the finances are sound and properly managed
- to ensure that resources are used efficiently and economically

As an employer

- to ensure that the organisation is a good employer to its paid and voluntary staff
- where paid staff are employed, to appoint the Director, and usually to be involved with the appointment of other senior staff
- to supervise and support the Director and ensure that other staff and volunteers are properly supervised

Evaluation

- to regularly monitor and evaluate the work of the organisation. This includes receiving reports from staff, staff supervision, getting feedback from clients and consumers, and so on

Insurance

- to make sure that the organisation is properly insured against all reasonable liabilities

Assets

- to make sure that any premises and equipment are properly looked after
- to ensure that investments and cash balances are managed properly

To be effective

- to work with the other committee members, to form an effective governing body for the organisation
- to attend meetings (and sub-committee meetings as appropriate), and to read papers in advance of meetings
- to participate in other tasks as arise from time to time, such as: interviewing new staff, helping with appeals and fundraising
- to keep informed about the activities of the organisation and about wider issues which affect its work
- to ensure that the organisation is effectively managed and gets its work done.

These tasks and duties are usually fulfilled by trustees meeting regularly to agree budgets, to review performance against budget, to supervise the running of the organisation, and (where there are no paid staff) to share out the responsibilities for getting things done.

> **"** I passionately believe that the trustees are there to make sure the proper processes are in place – such as for contracts. Trustees must be prepared to manage by process, not by task. Management and trustees are there to work together. Trustees must make sure that management comes to the right decisions, but not make them for them. So to be a trustee you must decide is the personal chemistry between you and the management team going to be right for you? Do you have a common aim? Do you feel a personal affinity for the organisation? Do you know your legal responsibilities? **"**
>
> Rodney Buse, Trustee and Chairman of Action Aid and Group Personnel Director, W H Smith

LIABILITIES OF TRUSTEES

The trustees are collectively responsible, and each trustee is personally responsible, for seeing that the organisation's affairs are in good order, that the charity operates within its constitution, and that it acts at all times in the interests of its beneficiaries.

Because this is a collective responsibility, trustees must share a sense of vision for the organisation, generally agree on how it does its work, and get on well together. It is also vital to have trustees with a range of skills.

" I didn't read any books or go on any courses to be a trustee. But we have always had an accountant and a lawyer to advise. These are the fundamentals to keeping the Trust properly organised. They are essential because there have often been times when there were legal or financial problems to deal with. The other trustees all have expertise of one form or another to contribute, and are people who want to give their own time to something in their local community. The majority of our trustees live or work within a mile of the Trust."

Gill Fitzhugh, Trustee, The Portobello Trust

Because trustees take personal responsibility, they must participate actively and keep themselves fully informed.

Not knowing what is going on, or not agreeing with a majority decision of the trustees, is no excuse. If the charity is found to be operating improperly, it is the responsibility of all the trustees. In such circumstances, the trustees would be 'in breach of trust'. If they are found not to have taken due care and attention or to be acting unreasonably, then they may find themselves personally liable for any loss. In cases of doubt or difficulty, proper advice may need to be obtained.

In charities with unincorporated legal status, the trustees are also personally liable for any debts, claims or breaches of contractual agreements, should the charity have insufficient assets to meet these. Where charities are constituted as companies limited by guarantee or as industrial and provident societies, the liabilities of trustees are limited to a nominal sum, normally £1. If the trustees are not protected, they can insure themselves against personal liability.

Trustees must understand not just their role and responsibilities, but also the potential liabilities that may arise from their trusteeship. However, personal liability is not normally a problem. Being a trustee is not all about undertaking onerous duties. It is usually a worthwhile and rewarding experience.

> **"** Being a trustee has given me a real insight into the lives and living conditions of the communities we serve and the complexities of running a highly motivated organisation. It has also given me a real and genuine sense of personal fulfilment and of doing something worthwhile. I have an inner belief that says it's people and working together jointly that matter. **"**
> Rodney Buse, Trustee and Chairman of Action Aid and Group Personnel Director, W H Smith

> **"** I really love being a trustee because of the people I work with across the board – the workers, the volunteers, the young people themselves and the employers. There is a sense of everyone working as a team in the same direction with common goals. And there is virtually no acrimony compared with my previous experience of working in an inner city school. Personally I get fulfilment and a sense of doing something worthwhile, but the main benefit is pleasure. Being a trustee is a very rewarding way of using your skills in a voluntary capacity. **"**
> Gill Fitzhugh, Trustee, Portobello Trust

FURTHER INFORMATION

The Charity Commission, 57-60 Haymarket, London SW1Y 4AY. This is the regulatory body for charities in England and Wales. It publishes a range of literature about charities and the roles and responsibilities of trustees.

National Council for Voluntary Organisations (NCVO), 8 All Saints Street, London N1 9RL. NCVO is the national agency promoting voluntary action. It has a special Trustee Services Unit dealing with trusteeship issues.

The Trustee Register, c/o Reed Charity Fund, 114 Peascod Street, Windsor SL4 1DN. People wishing to serve as charity trustees can put their name on the Register.

FURTHER READING

The Effective Trustee – a three-part guide to trusteeship. Part 1 covers roles and responsibilities, Part 2 deals with aims and resources, and Part 3 is about getting the work done. Each part costs £7.95 and is available from **Directory of Social Change**, Radius Works, Back Lane, London NW3 1HL.

15
VOLUNTEERING IN A CHARITY SHOP

Many of the very large charities and some local charities run charity shops. These are usually set up for fundraising purposes and sell mostly donated goods (including old clothes and bric-a-brac). Some shops have a section selling second-hand designer clothes for which there is a growing market. Usually these are donated, but some shops may be selling them on a commission basis for their owners. Other shops sell second-hand books and furniture.

Some voluntary organisations use their retail outlets to sell new products including:

- items manufactured by their beneficiaries (e.g. in a sheltered workshop or developing world project) e.g. straw baskets and hand-made goods
- items that they have specially produced, which promote the charity and its aims (e.g. **National Trust** shops selling their own branded goods)
- special lines that the buyer has been able to purchase cost effectively.

Charity shops selling mainly donated goods are offered certain VAT and rate reliefs. This means that many charity shops which sell new goods also will be selling donated goods alongside.

In addition, there are three chains of temporary shops operated by charities or charity consortia which sell charity Christmas cards in the run-up to Christmas each year (October-December).

The Growth of Charity Shops

The charity shop has become an important part of charity fundraising. Around 5,750 such shops were operating in the UK in 1992 with a turnover estimated at around £200 million. **Oxfam**, which set up its first shop over 25 years ago, now has 850 around the country – equivalent in number to well-known retail outlets such as Curry's or Dixons. Charities generally are picking up the idea; for example, **British Heart Foundation** had 15 shops in 1989 and now has over 120. **Imperial Cancer Research** has more than doubled its number of outlets over the past three years.

Rent and Staff

Many of the larger charities pay commercial rents or purchase their shop premises. Those shops run by smaller local charities often operate on a short-term basis at low or no rent taking over premises which would otherwise probably be empty. Many charity shops have a paid shop manager and some use volunteers or a mixture of volunteers and paid staff. Others rely entirely on volunteers.

What Jobs are there for Volunteers?

The jobs that need doing in a shop are very varied. Volunteers

- serve the public
- design window displays and devise ways of displaying the merchandise to its best effect
- work behind the scenes: stocktaking, ironing and sorting clothes and other goods
- undertake publicity for the shop and help to promote it locally.

The skills required will depend on what you do. But if you are working with customers or collecting stock from people's homes, you will need to be good with people, outgoing and personable, and generally a credit to the charity you are representing.

Why Volunteer?

This will depend on your circumstances:

- you may want retail experience and whatever training is offered
- you want to work and be part of the work environment
- you want somewhere to go and new people to meet
- you support the cause and want to make a worthwhile contribution.

Volunteering in an Oxfam Shop

"Our shops are an important way of generating revenue for Oxfam's overseas programme and emergency work. Volunteers contribute their time and talents in the shops, work in campaigns and undertake projects in our offices. We have over 26,000 volunteers who staff and operate 850 Oxfam shops in the United Kingdom and Ireland. Beyond a doubt they are our greatest resource.

Oxfam operates donated clothes shops, furniture shops and second hand book stores. Our volunteers are very creative and enterprising. One woman runs a very successful wedding gown rental service and donates the proceeds to Oxfam.

It can take from 30 to 60 volunteers to support an Oxfam shop depending on its size and location. They represent all age groups and backgrounds and offer a wide range of talents and skills. Volunteers provide support for Oxfam's programmes. We are all contributing something that is bigger than any of us.

People who are out of work or have been made redundant acquire experience or keep their skills from getting rusty by making a contribution of their time and energy while also looking for paid work.

Young people who have just left school or university can find the opportunity to acquire skills and get valuable work experience. They bring valuable energy and commitment.

Many retired people find that working in a shop provides the opportunity to apply their knowledge and experience while having stimulating contacts with the public and other volunteers"

Virginia Baird-Vivien, Volunteer Manager, Oxfam

How to volunteer:

- visit your local charity shop and ask about volunteering opportunities
- contact the Charity's Head Office and ask for a list of shops and what sort of needs they have for volunteer assistance.

As with all volunteer jobs, make sure you are clear about:
- the times and hours that are expected of you
- the tasks you will be performing
- the training and support that will be offered
- whether remuneration is offered for travel expenses, lunch etc.

Shops selling mainly Donated Goods

Charity	
Oxfam	850
Imperial Cancer Research	460
Sue Ryder Foundation	460
Barnardo's	290
Spastics Society	240
Age Concern	210
Cancer Research Campaign	200
British Red Cross	190
Help the Aged	180
Save the Children	160
Childrens Society	140
British Heart Foundation	120
Salvation Army	110
Helping Hand	70
MIND	70
Peoples Dispensary for Sick Animals	70
Shelter	70
RSPCA	50
National Children's Home	35
Notting Hill Housing Trust	30
NSPCC	30

Addresses and telephone numbers of the Head Office for each of these organisations can be found in either the *"Directory of Volunteering and Employment Opportunities"* (published by the Directory of Social Change) or the *"Voluntary Agencies Directory"* (published by the **National Council for Voluntary Organisations**).

Shops selling mainly Bought in Goods

National Trust 200
Royal National Lifeboat Institution (RNLI) 130
English Heritage 30
National Trust for Scotland 25
Royal Society for the Protection of Birds (RSPB) 25
Scout Association 20

Seasonal shops selling Charity Christmas Cards

- 1959 Group of Charities
- Card Aid (Charities Advisory Trust)
- 4Cs (Charity Christmas Card Council)

APPENDIX 1

ASSESSING YOUR SKILLS AND ATTRIBUTES

Many people possess skills and attributes which they don't recognise as important or useful. Carrying out your own **Skills and Attributes Audit**, perhaps with a friend, is a good way of finding these out – including all those you didn't know you had. This process will help you prepare your CV more effectively and decide which of your skills you most want to use and therefore the sort of position you would like, as well as helping you to choose the right charity to work for.

As a general rule, a skill is something you can DO and an attribute is something you ARE. The first step is to list all the skills you have, and give examples of them. Then think of the attributes you possess – which you were either born with or have developed as a result of life experience.

You may find it useful to think about your skills in various categories e.g. practical, pro-fessional, interpersonal.

- **Practical skills** might include: cooking, gardening, driving, sewing, knitting, carpentry
- **Professional skills** could include any qualifications you have e.g. a teaching diploma, a book-keeping certificate, a nursing degree; or any training courses you have taken such as National Vocational Qualifications (NVQs), City & Guilds etc. e.g. in office skills, word-processing, horticulture, catering
- **Inter-personal skills** might include caring for a family and bringing up children, the ability to cope in difficult circumstances or to listen to friends' problems, being a 'good neighbour'.

Attributes can include:

- patience
- perseverance
- understanding
- tolerance
- sense of humour
- flexibility
- creativity
- persuasiveness
- thoroughness
- initiative
- ability to cope in a crisis
- ability to be calm under pressure.

To help identify and define your skills and attributes, and the way you have applied them in practice, think about your life situation and the experiences you have had. Here are some examples:

You have managed a household – this has required:

- the ability to do 3 or more things at once!
- organisational and planning skills e.g. shopping, cooking, washing, cleaning
- being able to cook/sew/clean/etc.
- managing family life including timetables
- balancing budgets and housekeeping money

You've set up a Parent Teachers Association – this involved:

- getting people to help/join
- organisational skills such as arranging meetings
- drawing up a constitution
- persuading people to donate and getting funding
- planning agendas
- chairing meetings

You've worked as a volunteer with a telephone helpline – for this you have needed:

- counselling knowledge
- listening skills
- psychological insight
- tolerance and patience
- the ability to be non-judgemental

You've worked in a Bank for 30 years and been made redundant – you have experience in:

- financial skills – understanding ledgers, accountancy packages etc.
- money management including achieving branch targets
- managing staff
- dealing with many types of people from board members to the general public, some of whom can be difficult
- taking executive decisions
- coping with new technology and the changes it brings.

You are still at school and are wondering what you have to contribute. You may have:

- helped with producing a school magazine
- been involved with running a club or society
- done some fundraising for a charitable cause
- taken part in organising a community event e.g. fun run, summer fair
- argued for an issue you really believe in at a school debate.

You will probably find that you have many more skills and attributes, and much wider experience in using and applying them, than you thought. There will be some, if not all, that the voluntary sector can use. Good luck in your search for the right organisation.

APPENDIX 2

How to Write a Successful CV

For all job seekers a well-presented CV is vital in order to progress from applicant to interviewee. It is your primary marketing tool and you should be prepared, if necessary, to re-write, or angle it differently, for each job you apply for.

If you have never put together a CV before, you may like to turn to the preceding appendix "Assessing Your Skills and Attributes". When you have done this process, make sure your CV reflects the skills and attributes you possess. You may wish to illustrate each job, whether paid or voluntary, or each life-situation with two or three bullet points, saying what you have learnt.

Bear in mind that most people recruiting staff spend less than a minute looking at a CV before deciding whether or not to look further. Therefore make it as easy to read as possible. The front page is very important. It should:

- be easy to read, i.e. typed in a clear typeface
- contain your personal details: name, address, contact number and date of birth
- show recent work experience first, unless there is some special reason to 'star' something in the past
- show qualifications – in general only include the highest as further information can come later.

Make sure you include any voluntary work. Describe your volunteer job in the same way you would any other job.

It is a good idea not to exceed two sides of typed A4 paper. The object is not to provide an exhaustive survey of your life but to lead the reader into wanting to find out more about you, and into feeling that you could well be right for the organisation and the specific job.

You may need to come to terms with parts of your career history/life/education that make you feel uncomfortable or inadequate. This is particularly important if you are applying for a job following a redundancy or returning to work after bringing up a family. Present all this in as positive a light as possible. Most voluntary organisations are looking for people who are mature and flexible in their approach. Support from a friend or a 'buddy' can be particularly useful here. They may be able to identify aspects of you, your personality, your skills and your experience which you are blind to.

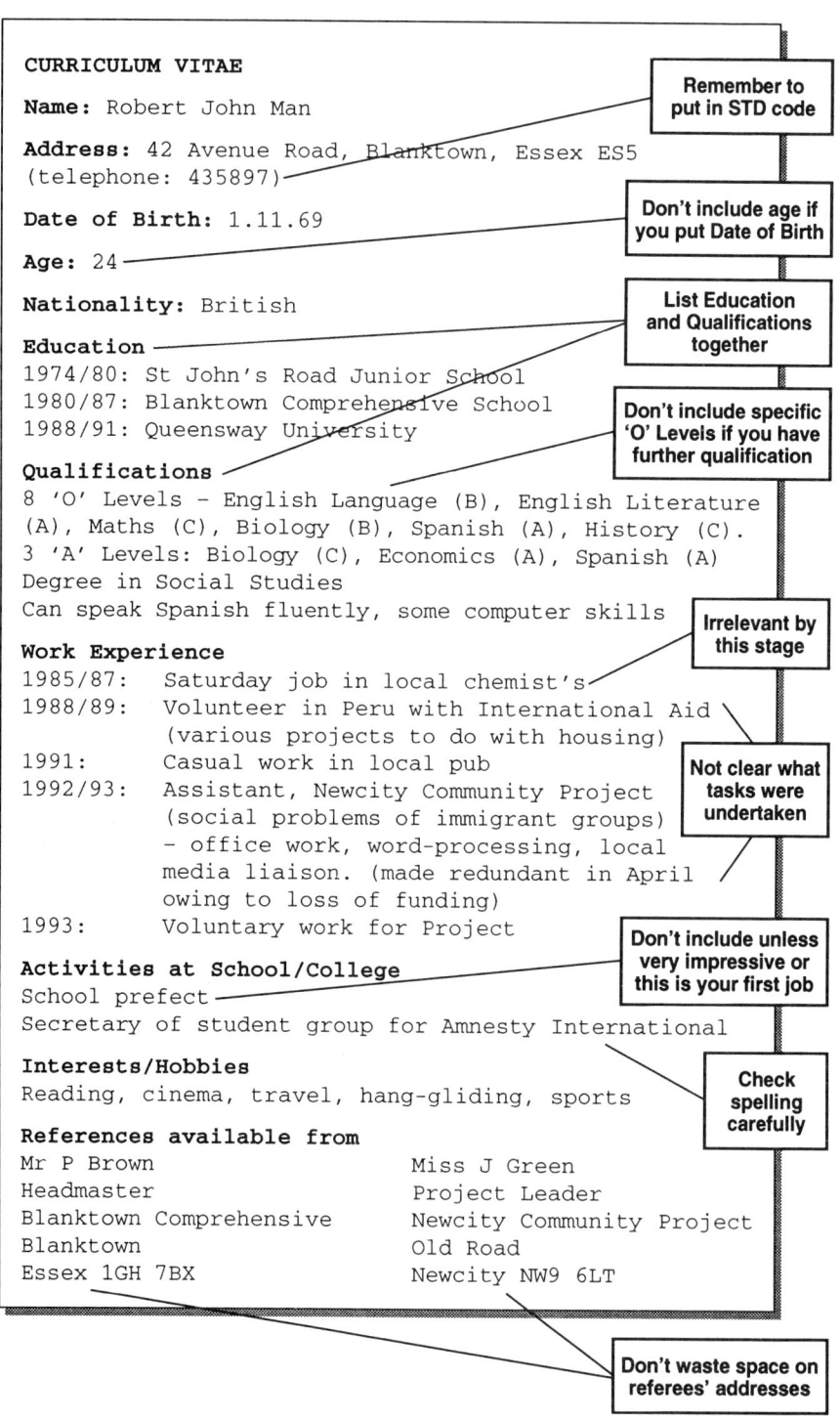

CURRICULUM VITAE

First impression – professional, easy to read, positive

PERSONAL DETAILS

Name	**Robert John Man**
Address	42 Avenue Road, Blanktown, Essex ES5
Telephone	0171-435897
Date of Birth	1 November 1969
Nationality	British
Languages	Fluent Spanish
Computer skills	Microsoft Word, MacWrite

Use bold type selectively for emphasis

Date written out in full for clarity

*Emphasize language skills – use words like **fluent, conversational***

Be specific about your computer skills

EDUCATION

1980–87:	Blanktown Comprehensive School 8 'O' Levels 3 'A' Levels: Biology (C), Economics (A), Spanish (A)
1987–88	Gap year – volunteer work in Peru
1988–91	Queensway University BSc, Social Studies – 2 (ii)

Gap year made very clear

WORK EXPERIENCE

January 1992 – April 93
Assistant, Newcity Community Project, Newcity

Skills / Achievements
- word-processing and office skills
- understanding of specific problems faced by immigrant communities
- experience with local media – newspapers, community radio

(Position ended in April 93 owing to loss of funding – since then worked on project as a volunteer 2 days a week)

Work experience in reverse order

Bullet point skills & achievements

Positive way of putting redundancy – shows commitment

October 1987– June 88
Volunteer, International Aid

Gap year spent working in Peru on housing project in Lima. Gained first-hand experience of poverty and social problems in a developing world country.

Make the most of any volunteer work

Interests

Reading, cinema, travel, hang-gliding, sports, international Justice issues

References – available on request

You can practice explaining the parts you feel most vulnerable about to each other – until the feeling of vulnerability goes.

If you have any glowing reference, endorsement or other 'third party' material extolling your virtues, it might be a good idea to attach a copy of this to your CV.

Having said all this, however, you may find a perfectly successful way of preparing a CV which breaks all the rules! The following sample CV should not be taken literally. It is an indication of ideas which have worked well for other people.

Useful Words for your CV

- Achieved
- Accountable
- Activity
- Analysis
- Charity
- Competent
- Communication
- Co-ordinated
- Costed
- Created
- Developed
- Effective
- Efficient
- Established
- Experience
- Improvement
- Initiated
- Maintained
- Managed
- Monitored
- Organised
- Positive
- Produced
- Professional
- Qualified
- Required
- Resources
- Responsible
- Set up
- Successful
- Trained
- Voluntary
- Volunteered
- Volunteering